PATRIOTS:

PROFILES OF EMINENT GAMBIANS

Hassoum Ceesay

Global Hands Publishing
2015

Patriots: Profiles of Eminent Gambians is published by:

Global Hands Publishing
Suite 1, Racial Equality Centre
5-9 Upper Brown Street,
Leicester
LE1 5TE
Tel: 01162577952
Email: publishing@global-hands.co.uk
Web: www.global-hands.co.uk

Typeset and Editing by Katie Gillatt, Global Hands Publishing
Cover Design and Illustration by: Daniel Sturrock

A CIP catalogue record for this book is available from the British Library.

ISBN: 978-0-9574073-6-7

ABOUT THE AUTHOR

Hassoum Ceesay is a highly regarded Gambian historian and literary critic.

He specialises in Gambian women's history and has published a widely acclaimed book titled *Gambian Women: An Introductory History.* His second book, titled *Gambian Women: Notes and Historical Profiles,* came out in 2011 and has received positive reviews.

Ceesay was features editor at the *Daily Observer* newspaper in Banjul, The Gambia, and was also editorial writer from 1999-2006. He currently works at the National Centre for Arts and Culture and is also Vice-President of the Writers Association of The Gambia.

This work is dedicated to Haddy Mbombeh, Assan and Habib (1982-2008)

Table of Contents

INTRODUCTION

This book seeks to interpret Gambia's past through the profiles of eminent men and women whose deeds have helped shape Gambian history. Historians continue to debate whether people or events shape history. And also if people shape history; is it the elite or the ordinary people who are most critical in shaping history? These debates will surely linger on, and they must not deflect practitioners of the discipline from giving players in the evolution of our country their rightful places in its history. This is what inspires me in this ambitious work.

Justification

The overwhelming majority of the published works on the history of The Gambia are general studies which seek to cover numerous events and epochs instead of focusing on specific episodes and persons. One result of this is that individuals who have helped to bend the arch of Gambian history do not get specific mentions in the form of profiles. This is a gap which needs to be filled. In other words, there has as yet been no attempt to use what Michel Doortmont calls the 'historical biography' genre to explain aspects of Gambian history.[1]

This work seeks to fill the gap of biographical material in Gambian history. This is important because the history of any society simultaneously tells us the stories of the lives and times of the main characters of that society and particular period. While it is true that communities mould people, so do people also shape the fortunes of those communities. We need to study the careers of such people in order to fully appreciate our history. Moreover, works such as this also help to build role models to inspire our youth into gainful and patriotic actions.

---

[1] Doormont,M. *The Pen-Pictures by Charles Francis Hutchinson*, Brill, 2005, p.36-40

The Gambian men and women profiled here belonged to and operated in different milieu, contexts and epochs: the pre-colonial, colonial and post-colonial eras, for example. Therefore, it would be quite unfair to use the historian's license of judgment and verdict on them; instead, we shall measure what they have achieved against the odds stacked against them. Yet from the evidence I have presented, it is clear that they were patriots to the core who cared for the welfare of their people and did their best to mould a better Gambia amidst the uncertainty and subjugation of colonial rule or the lean and uncertain times of post-independence. On the whole, the life stories here are tales of victory over adversity; of triumph over uncertainty. My aim remains to drag the characters from historical oblivion and shift them from marginalia to the centre spread of Gambian history.

Scope

Every attempt has been made to discuss the characters in the full context of Gambian history so as not to isolate them as if they were acting in a historical void. The scope covers the period from the 1700s, when the present day entity called The Gambia was a series of independent states ruled by powerful sovereigns with advanced administrative, political and economic set ups, to the present times. The characters in this book were born, matured and accomplished their callings within this odd 400 years period. Even then, there are only 40 out of possible hundreds of achieving Gambians discussed in this book. I chose characters whose lives could be more easily assembled or reconstructed using the various sources at my disposal. I challenge other historians to pick up the baton from here and research into the life stories of other Gambian patriots, and possibly, villains. I have included people from various works of life: traditional authorities, journalists, cultural workers, politicians and ordinary Gambians. Women have also been given a fair representation to make the book more inclusive.

I wish to also suggest to the reader to consult my two earlier books: *Gambian Women: Introductory History* (Fulladu Publishers, 2008, 2013) and *Gambian Women: Profiles and Historical Notes* (Fulladu Publishers, 2010), both of which carry profiles of eminent Gambian women achievers. In a series of entries in the Oxford University *Dictionary of African Biography* (2010, 2013), and the *Oxford African American Studies Centre,* I have also profiled a number of Gambian achievers in different spheres of life. Indeed, my interest in interpreting Gambian history through the lenses of its great men and women knows no bounds. This choice is deliberate. Because I subscribe to the assertion that 'the biographical sphere is by it's very nature interdisciplinary, because a single historical biography borders on many other genres, subjects and narrative traditions; it raises the issues of politics, social relations, economics, and culture, ancestry, kinship, family, sexuality, psychology, and friendship'.[2] Therefore, through biographical profiles, we can reconstruct a person's contributions to all of society's spheres during their life time and even beyond.

Methodology

The profiles are arranged in a chronological order which is why Fenda Lawrence, the 18th century trader, leads the pack. The lengths of the profiles do not indicate a scale of significance, but rather the corpus of material available to me during the research. Most of the research was archival. During a research trip to the UK in the summer of 2008, I was able to unearth lots of primary materials from the British Archives, and I have also dug into the Gambia National Archives, especially newspapers such as the *Gambia Echo, Gambia News Bulletin* and the *Gambia Outlook.* I have done oral interviews with family members and some of the players

---

[2] See Possing, B. 'Biography: Historical' in www.possing.dk/pdf/historicalbio.pd ***accessed 1/11/15***

themselves; secondary material gleamed from authoritative sources, such as Hughes and Perfect's dependable *Historical Dictionary* of the Gambia (2008) also proved useful. Like any other researcher, I had to confront the lack of adequate resources and time, but thanks to numerous well-wishers these issues were overcame.

Special thanks go to Ousainou Jagne of Timbooktoo for his support and understanding, and to my family and colleagues at the National Centre Arts Culture, especially Mr.Baba Ceesay for his support. I also extend thanks to Dr. Momodu Sallah, Dr. Ebrima Ceesay, Dr. Jeggan Senghor, Dr. Cymore Fourshey, Dr Toby Green, Professor Judith Carney, and Richard Rosamoff, Nana Grey-Johnson, Dr. Cherno Omar Barry, Dr. A. A. Sengor, Dr. Pierre Gomez, Alhaji A.M Sering-Secka for their many years of academic partnership, and to the staff at Global Hands Publishing for the professional touch they have given the book.

Fenda Lawrence (1742-1800): Merchant, Émigré

Before delving into the interesting life story of this eighteenth century pioneer woman trader, it is vital to assess the conditions that prevailed in The Gambia during the period to help us better situate her lifetime. Politically, the era was marked by intense rivalry among the major European nations that had trading presence in the River Gambia, namely, the French, British and Dutch. This rivalry was mainly premised on trading rights, but also for political control over the trading centres such as Fort James Island and Albreda[3]. The rivalry was so

---

1. See Georgia Ashcraft-Eason, L. 'She voluntarily hath come: a Gambian woman trader in Colonial.' in *Identity in Shadow of Slavery*, Paul E Lovejoy (ed), Continuum, London and New York, 2000, pp.202-218. This is a well-argued essay, which, though thin on evidence on the life of Fenda particularly her later years in the US, gives a thorough argument on the subject. My thanks go to Judith Carney for introducing me to the work. See also Bennet Jr, L. *Before the Mayflower: A History of the Negro in America (1619-1966)*,

intense that wars fought between these nations in faraway Europe spilled over into the River Gambia area. Fort James became the theatre of this inter-European warring over trade and political rights. The most significant political development to arise out of this rivalry was the creation of the short-lived province of Senegambia in 1765. It brought together the British possessions of Gorée, St Louis and James Island under crown rule led by an executive governor and assisted by a council of advisers. The erudite Gambian historian Dr. Florence Mahoney states that the province was the first experience in crown colony rule in Africa, and its constitution that provided for a governor and a council became the model system of governance during colonial rule. The province was however short-lived; it was built on conquest, and lost to

---

Johnson Publishing, Chicago, 1966, p.41. The certificate of passage issued by the Governor of Georgia states: '*(Fenda) is a free black woman and heretofore-a considerable trader in the River Gambia on the coast of Africa (who) hath voluntarily come to be and remain for sometime in this province.*' The Governor gave orders that she should be allowed to 'pass unmolested within the state' while doing her legitimate business.

conquest. When Britain lost the American War of Independence in 1778, the French, who supported the American revolutionaries, regained the territories they lost and the province collapsed. However, the brisk trade in slaves and legitimate items continued to flourish among the Africans, European and Mullato traders in the factories along the river. The social milieu was indeed multi-ethnic, with many of the trade centres such as Bintang and Albreda inhabited by Africans and several other populations. The situation in The Gambia at the time was a recipe for economic intermingling and social acculturation.

Fenda was born around 1742 to a Serahule family that lived in the Kingdom of Wuli, in the upper limits of the River Gambia. Fenda was described as 'a black, free woman of material substance, a considerable slave trader', who lived in Kaur, in the central reaches of the River Gambia. She migrated to Georgia, USA, in May 1772 in search of a better life and more lucrative trade. Her father worked at British-owned factories at Wulitenda,

Doomasansang, Bansang Tenda and later, Carrol's Wharf, in Nianija, while her mother worked as a maid for white traders. She therefore grew up in the multi-cultural business environment of the factories along the river, which had mulatto, European and African populations. This shaped her life. Furthermore, the numerous successful mulatto women traders who operated up river must have inspired Fenda into trading. Although she was not of mixed race, she nonetheless belonged to the signara class because of her wealth and marriage to a European trader.[4]

In 1760, she married an Englishman James Lawrence, who was the employer of her parents at Kaur. As her husband was away most of the time up river negotiating trading rights with chiefs, Fenda ran the businesses at Kaur and Nianimaro. She used this chance to build up her network of business contacts in the region.

---

[4] Women of mullato stock who wielded much influence and wealth in the 16th to 19th centuries in the Senegambia area, see Ceesay, H. *Gambian Women: An Introductory History, Fulladu Publishers*, 2007.

In 1780, her husband died leaving her with three children. She was now to take charge of his vast business concerns along the river, which included three shallops that plied the river ports transporting goods and slaves. However, Fenda was unable to remain a successful trader because local chiefs and armed marauders coerced her into surrendering her fortune. She lost her boats to the king of Wuli, who sold them off to a French trader based in Albreda. Also, her own parents forced her to yield much of her business to them. Lilian Ashcraft-Eason has suggested that 'patriarchal, paternalistic and communal tendencies within the Kingdom of Saloum' (where Kaur was located) could have interfered with Fenda's business in Kaur as the *alkali* and local chiefs questioned her dower rights or for other reasons withdrew their support.[5] Fenda would have had a problem because under both local law and Islamic law, wives could not inherit their husbands' property. Traditionally, when a foreigner like Fenda's

[5] See Georgia Ashcraft-Eason. L. *Identity in Shadow of Slavery, p.202-218.*

husband died, the local chiefs had the right to claim their property.

Whatever might have pushed her out of her homeland to the Americas, Fenda left Kaur with her family aboard a slave ship called *New Britannia* in 1792 and arrived in Georgia, an exile determined to succeed. With the help of contacts she knew while in Kaur, she soon obtained full residency status, and gained acquaintances with the trade community of Savannah, the main trade centre of Georgia in the 18th century. She bought and resold slaves and also traded in cotton, such that she began to make profits. Before she died, Fenda had built a huge trading concern in Georgia and other southern states.

Fenda's achievements were indeed substantial for an African woman of the 18th century. She was able to use her contacts with Europeans to develop business, but has been criticized for profiting in slave trading. However, her business success in Georgia opened the door for more African women to follow her footsteps and migrate to the Americas to pursue trade, among them Liz Hoffman, a Sierra Leonean woman. Fenda was a major player in the period in history Ashcraft-Eason called 'an irrational proto-capitalist era,' when strength and ruthlessness were needed to succeed in commerce. She was simply a success-driven Gambian woman, who used the opportunities presented to her to make money and live a happy life. Her movement to America shows that while the majority of Blacks by the middle of the nineteenth century reached the New World aboard the ignominious slave ships that plied the Middle Passage, another notable group came as free persons establishing themselves as viable entrepreneurs.

Kemintang Kamara (1770- 1841): King of Upper Niani and Anti-Colonial Leader

In 1835, a Niani King named Kemintang Kamara inflicted the first major defeat against the British colonial forces at a battle near his capital at Dungaseen and became the undisputed anti-colonial ruler in the upriver regions of The Gambia. This military defeat angered and embarrassed the British so much that their Governor in Bathurst, George Rendall, was recalled and later dismissed. Kemintang went to war to protect his trade and political rights against British aspirations.

In 1834, he had seized a river cutter called 'ORA' belonging to a big Bathurst merchant named William Goddard in retaliation to a trading agent of Goddard's in Tendaba, Saloum Jahateh, seizing two of Kemintang's relatives after a dispute over a debt[6]. Apparently, Goddard had also refused to pay his annual tax to Kemintang for the right to trade in Niani Kingdom which included the areas covered by the present day districts of Sami, Niani and Nianija in the Central River Region. Goddard complained to Governor Rendall who chose to forcefully ask Kemintang to return the vessel. Kemintang refused, and the British dispatched a 120 men force to attack Kemintang. Rendall attacked because he had just received reinforcement of officers and men in the war boat BRISK from Sierra Leone. Additionally, local chiefs hostile to Kemintang were in mutiny and this induced him to attack. Furthermore, the merchants of Bathurst had come forward and contributed money to help Rendall's war effort; other merchants like Thomas Joiner volunteered to spy on Kemintang's forces. Rendall was additionally able to get allies in Jimara to join him in the battle against Kemintang. By May 1835, Rendall was able

---

[6] See Huntley, H. *Seven Years on the Slave Coast of Africa*, London, 1841, p.275-277. See also Hughes, A, and David Perfect. *Historical Dictionary of The Gambia'*, London, 2008, p.129.

to mobilise a huge arsenal ready to attack Kemintang: two war ships, the REFORM and the VICTOR; a patrol boat, fifty volunteers, militia stationed at Maccarthy Island, one howitzer gun, two cannons, twelve field rockets, and over six hundred foot soldiers and eight boats loaded with ammunition and provisions.

On his part, Kemintang built a huge defensive moat, and an extra defence of a mud wall in front of a strong stockade fence. Inside the stockade, he collected grain and other provisions sufficient to withstand a long siege. He mobilised an army of two thousand men and infiltrated the enemy by having a fifth column planted inside the British forces. From May 30th to June 1st 1835, the two armies fought a massive battle near Dungaseen. The British forces and their allies failed to breach the defensive fort after a day of pounding with rockets. In addition, half of the British allies' forces from Jimara had disappeared into the forest as they approached Dungaseen, thanks to infiltration by Kemintang's spies. Also, Kemintang had poisoned the streams and wells along the path of the invading British army such that they had no access to water. By the second day, Kemintang had killed half the invading forces, and captured a big arsenal of howitzers and rockets. Governor Rendall was wounded and many of his commanders captured. Kemintang however, did not finish off the retreating British army; instead, he allowed them to escape back to Maccarthy Island[7].

His war against the British was one of 'several acts of military resistance mounted by Gambian rulers against European infiltration into their territories. Others wars included: the Barra war of 1831, the Battle of Toubabkolong of 1866 and the Sankandi incident of 1900 when irate villagers killed several British officials and soldiers'.[8]

---

[7] See CSO 1/4 Rendall to Colonial Secretary, 7 June 1834, for a blow by blow account of the battle. See also Ceesay, H. 'Kemintang Kamara' *African American Studies Center* http://www.oxfordaasc.com/article/opr/t356/e0049 (accessed Fri Feb 14 14:24:32 EST 2014).

[8] See Ceesay, H. 'Kemintang Kamara', *African American Studies Center*

'Kemintang's defeat of the British made him the undisputed leader of Niani and he regained the rights of taxing merchants who traded beyond Macarthy Island'.[9] To cover the shame of their defeat, the British accused Kemintang of devil worship and human sacrifice to propitiate the gods. The defeated Rendall spread the news that before the battle, Kemintang had slaughtered a pageant of virgins in idol worship. This was subterfuge at best; Kemintang won the war due to superior tactics and had he pursued the fleeing British, not a single soldier would have escaped to Bathurst to tell the tale of defeat. Instead, he contented himself with seizing their stores, guns and ammunition, which he later proudly mounted at his town's square, as he was unable to operate them.

---

http://www.oxfordaasc.com/article/opr/t356/e0049 (accessed Fri Feb 14 14:24:32 EST 2014

[9] Ceesay, H. 'Kemintang Kamara', Oxford African American Studies Centre.

Before Kemintang's war with the British, he had solidified his position as overlord of Niani by killing Namory Sabbaly, King of Kataba at a battle in Dini Kunda near Kai hai Island, opposite Kunatur in 1824. The Kataba King was getting too close to the British, who then attempted to convert the king to Christianity. When that failed, the British coaxed him to send one of his sons to the school at Georgetown. A Kataba-British alliance was cold comfort to Kemintang, who struck first and overran Kataba, capturing the population as slaves and annexing the territory. The loss of a potential ally miffed the British, and this explains their antagonism against the Niani king.

Kemintang died in 1841 and was replaced by Koliba Sabally as king of Niani. Kemintang epitomized the fierce spirit of independence that rulers in upriver states possessed at the dawn of British imperialism in the River Gambia areas in the early 19th century. Even his enemies could not but appreciate his military prowess. 'He is a formidable antagonist…a brave warrior… a man of colossal stature and great courage' wrote Governor Huntley of Bathurst in 1837.[10]

[10] See Huntley, 257.

Sheikh Mass Kah (1827-1936): Religious Scholar and Saint

According to the 2003 census, ninety five per cent of Gambians profess the Islamic faith[11]. Except in Banjul, the capital, and its outlying districts, the rest of the country is predominantly Muslim. Islam in The Gambia dates back to the 1550s. European explorers like Richard Jobson were describing Muslims, Islamic rites and dress in the areas along the River Gambia[12]. Islam came to the Gambia through Trans Saharan trade routes that were the commercial axis between North Africa and West Africa. As early as the 11th century, the rulers of Futa Toro to the North of The Gambia, had been converted to Islam by their trade partners; in the same century the Almoravids were converting by the sword or the bushel, peoples of Southern

[11] Gambia Census data, 2003, Gambia Bureau of Statistics.
[12] See Gamble, D. and PEH Hair. *The Voyages of Richard Jobson* (Hakylut Society)London: 2002)

Mauritania. It was the Futa Toro and Mauritanian Muslims that brought Islam southwards to the River Gambia Region. Hunwick[13] asserts that the Almoravids implanted the first seeds of Islam in the Senegambia region, mainly their Malilki school of Thought. Sanneh[14] and Robinson[15] note that the Jula traders, itinerant Manding merchants who were major partners in the Trans Saharan Trade, were the agents for the rapid Islamisation of The Gambia. However, the most significant transmitters of Islam and Islamic culture were the clerics who were working in the courts of the states of The Gambia such as Kaabu, Niumi, and Saloum. As they were close to the centres of power, they had much influence in the conversion of the rulers and also ordinary people.

---

[13] Hunwick, J. 'Sub Saharan Africa and the Wider World of Islam" Journal of Religion in Africa, 26, 3 (1966): P.232

[14]Sanneh, L., 'Futa Jallon and the Jahanke Clerical Tradition'. Part 1: the Historical Setting: Journal of Religion in Africa, 12, (1981):P. 38-64. See also Sanneh, L. ' *Jahanke: Muslim Clerics: A religious and Historical Study of Islam in Senegambia*, (Lantham: University of America Press, 1989). In this book , Professor Sanneh investigates the identity of Jahanke Muslim Clerics, whose significance in the Islamisation of much of pre-colonial West Africa is without parallel.

Sheikh Mass Kah was born of Fulbe origin in Ngui Mbayen in the Wollof state of Kayoor in present day Senegal in 1827 and died in the Gambia in 1936 at the village of Medina Sering Mass, in the Niumi District of The Gambia[16]. His father was Ma Sohna Kah and his mother was Sohna Gaye Khan. He lost his parents at a young age and grew up under foster parents. As was customary at the time, Mass Kah went to Quranic school, or d*aara,* in the University town of Piir in present day Senegal. Piir was the school where many Islamic reformers studied and Mass Kah must have met many other clerics from Futa Toro and Middle Senegal. He also studied in Mauritania under the renowned Sheikh Sidiya at Boutilmit. When he returned home, he began to attract scholars and followers by his peaceful approach to Islam. His gentle stance was a pragmatic approach as by this time, militant Islam was in decline because the French, in their imperial designs, had defeated or accommodated the jihadist like Lat Jorr and Maba Jahou Bah.

---

[16] Interview with Imam Muhamadu Lamin Bah, Serekunda, The Gambia, May 2001.

Therefore, he saw reason in spreading the Word of Allah by teaching and avoiding any confrontation with the Europeans.

Mass Kah's attitude towards the colonial powers was total avoidance. Thus, whenever the French or British authorities came close to his establishment, he would relocate to a new place. This is why he had lived in Karang, Amdalaye (border towns of Senegal and Gambia), Bathurst (Banjul) and Media Sering Mass. According to oral traditions, his motto was "If you cannot agree with the ruler [Europeans], you have to leave his land for him". In so doing, he avoided conflict with the colonial rulers and protected himself and followers from destruction. A good example of such tactical removal was his establishment of the clerical village of Medina Sering Mass Kah named after him in the 1890s, which today remains a renowned Muslim village. He established the village in his own image, that is, to teach the Quran, to spread the Word of Allah, and to do agriculture work. He therefore, stressed the two fundamental principles of hard work and religious piety.

The school he built at the village attracted students from everywhere. The school grew so big that it soon attracted the attention of the Colonial Travelling Commissioner of North Bank Province. In his report for 1923, he noted: "there are a number of schools at which Arabic is taught, chiefly that of Mass Kah... some of the teachers are highly educated men.."[17]

Muhamed Joof in his study of Islamic schools in West Africa notes the schools run by Mass Kah as centres of excellence in Quranic education[18]. By establishing schools, he was fulfilling many roles: chiefly, he was spreading Islam by peaceful means during a turbulent period where most others were spreading Islam by the use of horse and the sword. Thus he was emphasizing the values of peaceful

---

[17] Travelling Commissioner Report for North Bank Province, 1925, Gambia National Archives.,

[18] Joof, M. *History of Islamic Schools in West Africa.* Dakar: Koki, 1996, pp113-114.

coexistence[19] whilst promoting literacy for the masses and empowering them for the future. Furthermore, by establishing schools, Islamic clerics, like him, obtained a larger number of followers and gained the trust and confidence of the communities, enriching and adding value to the lives of the people.

The Sheikh's ability to draw divine inspiration to alter circumstances in favour of those of his followers in disadvantageous positions also added to his prestige. In some ways, these gestures by the Sheikh illustrate how he reached out to the ordinary people around him and how he responded to their daily worries especially when they came into collision with the new colonial laws and regulations at the turn of the 19th century. This miraculous intervention made the Sheikh relevant to the communities and was able to draw and maintain new followers. Above all, he put a lid on

[19] Interview with Chernor Kah, Quranic teacher, Medina Daru Seringe Mass, Niumi, October 2010. I thank Dr. Bala Saho, now at Oklahoma State University, who introduced me to this eminent scholar and saint, and whose work on Sheikh Mass Kah have drawn from.

social tensions as he was able to give hope to the despairing masses.

Yet, the disciples had to give something in return: farm work and free labour. One could argue that the teachings of Islam provided clerics with the ideological base upon which they could exploit the labour of their disciples, since in Islam it appears that there is a link between work for elders and clerics and blessings. Students would join a daara not merely to learn the Quran but also to work the fields for their teacher. Gamble[20] notes that the cleric appears like "a man without needs, indifferent to material things, yet whose basic needs for food, shelter, clothes and housing would be taken care of by the disciples" through farm labour. Sheikh Mass Kah's disciples worked his farms to sustain themselves and his family. This was their duty to him to requite his protection, support and blessings. Indeed, the proceeds from

---

[20] Gamble, D.__*Peoples of The Gambia: The Wollof*, San Francisco: Gambian Studies No. 17. See also, Saho, B. *Personhood: The Life Times of Sering Mass Kah*, DBC Printers, 2009 for details on the Sheikh life and work..

the farm were so big that the Sheikh's granary was like an emergency food reserve from which the community could draw from in times of need. Thus hunger and its attendant problems such as social conflict were put at bay.

Musa Molloh (1872-1931) King of Fulladu, Anti-Colonial Resistance Leader

David Perfect and Arnold Hughes in their authoritative book *Historical Dictionary of The Gambia* (2008) called him 'the son of Alfa Molloh, founder of the Fula kingdom of Fulladu'[21]. To this modest introduction we must add that he was a Muslim Fula, the second ruler of the Empire of Fuladu, a skilled diplomat who played the British against the French to strengthen his position. Fuladu was part of the Fula Confederation that stretched from The Gambia River to the Corubal River in Guinea Bissau and incorporated both British and French territory.

---

[21] See Hughes, A. and David Perfect. *Political History of The Gambia 1816-1994*, University of Rochester Press, (2008) p.147.

Raiders were annually sent in to invade the Upper River Area because this region was under the control of exiled Marabouts who were previously part of the confederation. Shortly after Musa Molloh was born, Alfa Molloh began his uprising (1867-68) against animist Mandinka neighbours who were persecuting the Fula population. Part of his military efforts included establishing Islam wherever he gained control.

Alfa Molloh died in 1874 and was succeeded by his brother, Bakary Demba, who was to bequeath the throne to Musa Molloh. Disputes arose over the inheritance but Musa Molloh decided to recognise his uncle as overlord, although for the next decade there were conflicts between the two. Aware of the dangers of civil war, Musa Molloh went south of the Casamance. After Bakary Demba's death in 1884, Musa Molloh became sole ruler of Fuladu. He became a very useful ally for the British, French and local West African Government in The Gambia as he acted as mediator between various groups when trying to settle ethnic differences. In 1887

Molloh assisted the French against Momodou Lamin Drammeh, a Soninke marabout who was rebelling against foreign domination. In the 1890's Musa Molloh strategised to consolidate his power when he co-operated with the British in fighting against Fode Kabba, an extremely powerful marabout and war leader based in the Kombos who was one of the last opponents of colonial rule.

By 1892 Musa Molloh proclaimed himself supreme ruler throughout all of British and French Fuladu. His territory lay on both sides of the arbitrary colonial boundaries but he lived on the French side. In 1901 he handed over control of British Fuladu to the Government of The Gambia. This transfer made possible the British administration of the protectorate system for all of The Gambia except St. Mary's Island. For ceding his territory, he was granted chief status and given an annual subvention of five hundred pounds a year.

An ordinance of 1902 incorporated Fuladu into the colony which halted the slave trade that Musa

Molloh was still engaged in. Two years later, feeling pressured by French colonial interests and being accused of tyrannical conduct, Musa Molloh retreated to British territory and settled in Kesser Kunda near Georgetown. Not appreciating his autocratic manner and urged on by the allegations of his enemies, the British exiled Musa Molloh to Sierra Leone in 1919. Exile abroad and banishment to a remote corner of The Gambia were two ways of punishment for chiefs who were out of favour with the colonial authorities during colonial rule. Both meant complete sequestration from family and loss of property. In 1920, the records show that Musa was able to negotiate from exile the sale of his house at Kesserkunda for one hundred pounds to the British who brought it down and used the material to build a rest house in Bansang. They also distributed his many wives to his friends and foes. They were determined to remove any trace of him.

The decision by Governor Ed Cameroon to send Musa into exile was a controversial one which raised eye brows even at the British Commons.

Many saw it as an arbitrary decision done without recourse to a public trial. Asked why Musa was exiled to Freetown, the British Under Secretary of State for the Colonies retorted:

> Musa Molloh is being deported because it was found that he was in the habit of keeping a large number of women in a condition of slavery'. No formal trial was held but the matter was very fully investigated by the Governor and his officers and Musa Molloh had the opportunity of explaining his conduct, if it had been susceptible of any satisfactory explanation.

This was unsatisfactory explanation for a lack of trial. The British public opinion was such that by 1923 mounting pressure had forced the colonial government to revoke the deportation and Musa returned but without any political power. He died at Kesser Kunda in 1931.

The accusations of slavery were also not trusted at least by traditional historians or griots including Bamba Suso, who narrated to the well informed Gambian historian Bakari Sidibe in the 1960s, the following defence of Musa's conduct:

> There were one hundred and twenty five women and children in Musa's compound. Not all of them were his wives. Kingship attracts people. Each wife would have brought with her either a relative or a slave or both to help her with her work, or as a link between her and her people. This was customary in the houses of prominent people. They were additional mouths to feed, but their contributions in labour and support were usually greater. Large compounds of this kind usually grew more food than they could consume themselves, and this food surplus was a factor, which attracted even more dependents. It is also a factor, which attracted families with marriageable daughters, looking for an

alliance with populous, well-fed households. Their behaviours does not indicate any existence of or expectations of cruel treatment[22].

In many ways, Suso's narration sounds more plausible for Musa's overcrowded palace than the Europeans' suspicion of a harem.

Musa Molloh, Foday Kaba and Foday Sillah were the political leaders who resisted the European penetration and annexation in the second half of the 19th century. They were particularly fired up to defend the independence of their states and economic interests. In many ways also, they were the role models for the nationalist politicians of the 1950s who based their anti-colonial stance on the earlier resistance exploits of Musa Molloh and his peers.

His son, Cherno Balde, was the final ruler of the Empire of Fuladu. Musa Molloh is renowned as a

[22] See Sidibe, B. *A History of Fuladu and Kaabu' 1300-1900*, L'Harmattan, Turin, 2005, p.150.

famous warrior and leader of troops as well as being a skilful diplomat in being able to deal successfully with both the French and British in the midst of Senegambian politics. His tomb at Kesserkunda, near Bansang, was restored in 1971 and was declared a National Monument in 1974.

Joseph Richards (1843-1917): Merchant and Nationalist Politician

Richards was born in Freetown in 1843, and moved to Bathurst with his parents at the age of two. He attended the Wesley School in Bathurst until 1862. Richards was a leading Gambian political activist, trader, and socialite best remembered for his dogged and persistent opposition to the many schemes hatched by Britain to cede or exchange Gambia for other French territories between 1867 and 1909. The first attempt was in February 1866 when the French Government proposed to Britain that The Gambia colony be exchanged for another French colony with similar size such as Gabon. Britain was no longer prepared to hold on to a colony it saw as too little endowed with resources to pay for its running costs. Local elites led by Joseph Richards immediately opposed this because they believed that a cession of Gambia to France would kill trade as the French would not allow free commerce. He led a massive petition campaign signed by hundreds of Gambians including chiefs, traders and market women in Bathurst. Richards, who wrote to many newspapers in England and the USA, condemned the proposed exchange and also took the protest to the wider world opinion.. Constant pressure from Richards forced the British to abandon the idea of cession in 1870[23].

However, four years later the idea of ceding Gambia to France again cropped up. Concerned with the worsening wars between the Soninke and the Marabouts in Kombo and Barra, and disturbed by the prospect of an attack from the Marabout armies on Bathurst, Britain intended to transfer Gambia to France. Again, Richards stuck to his guns and opposed the proposal. He established The Gambia Native Association which according to Hughes and Perfect (2010) included other patriots such as Harry Finden and Samuel Forster Snr., to

---

[23] See Florence, M. *Gambia Studies*, Banjul, 2006, p.162.

canalize opposition to the transfer scheme. Richards wrote a strong petition to the Colonial Secretary in London signed by 150 Gambians, detailing why they opposed the transfer to France. He noted that such a transfer would destroy Gambian identity, destroy the liberties they were enjoying under British rule and also jeopardise the future of their children. He touched a raw nerve in his petition when he highlighted the huge untapped potential of the River Gambia in trade, scientific research and agriculture which would be lost to Britain when the transfer went ahead. This particular point endeared him to many in the UK House of Commons who then opposed the cession move. Richards continued to oppose the 1904 and 1909 moves to transfer Gambian territory to France.

Richards had excelled as a legislator in Bathurst when in 1882, he was nominated as the first African to sit in the Legislative Council. The Legislative Council established in Bathurst in 1843, comprised of only Europeans during its first forty years[24]. Therefore, in Council he faced tremendous opposition from vested merchants' interest and those of the White members who saw him as an agitator for African rights. He frequently attacked Government policy towards the local people including the absence of educational opportunities and the exploitative work of the European firms. In 1888, he lost his seat and concentrated his efforts on business.

Richards was a major trading agent for big Bathurst firms like Forster and Smith and William Goddard, whom he represented upriver for many years. He later established his kola nut-trading firm which for many years monopolized the trade in the commodity. He amassed wealth and was able to build with imported bricks, the most expensive mansion 'Villa Itoko' in Albion Street in Bathurst, 1916, just a few months before his death.[25]. He died in Bathurst in 1917 and according to Florence

---

[24] See Mahoney, F. *Stories of Senegambia*, Banjul, 1982, p.83-84.

[25] See Hughes, and Perfect, *A Political History of The Gambia* , Scarecrow Press, 2006, p.69.

Mahoney his huge wealth was soon after dissipated by wrangling over inheritance by his sons. It is to his credit that The Gambia maintained her separate identity in the face of repeated attempts to transfer her to the French in the 19th century

Sir Samuel John Forster (1873-1940): First Gambian Lawyer

When Sir Samuel Forster died in July 1940, Governor Southern stated in his eulogy that he believed that it would be difficult to find suitable person to fill his seat in the Legislative Council and his other multifarious roles in the society[26]. While this statement angered some sections of the Bathurst intelligentsia, others tended to agree with it; for upon his death there was a strong feeling that Gambia's aspirations for political and social advancement would be jeopardized by the 'dearth of credible leaders'. This frustration was explained by Sir Samuel's wide ranging roles and activities in Bathurst society as a legislator, lawyer, journalist, nationalist politician, churchman and socialite. His

[26] See *Gambia Echo*, July 29 1940. See also Hughes and Perfect(2006) p.48, 76-78.

rich career was however, firmly anchored in a sound education and strong family pedigree.

He was born in 1873[27] to the Honourable Samuel Forster, a rich merchant and Gambian Legislative Council Member from 1886-1906. His mother Lucy Forster was a respected Aku woman who died in 1927 at the ripe old age of eighty four. Sir Samuel was one of twelve children born to the Forsters. Before dissecting his rich educational background, it is imperative to examine the political and social context of the 1870s in Bathurst colony under which Sir Samuel was born. Externally, the 1870s was a period of great uncertainty for the Colony of Bathurst as in 1873 the British started new negotiations with the French to exchange Gambia Colony with Gabon in Central Africa. The previous attempts to exchange Gambia for Senegal had failed due to stiff opposition from local chiefs, merchants and a few educated elite of Liberated Africans later called Aku. Thus when the British revived the exchange scheme, the African elites

---

[27] See Hughes and Perfect, *Historical Dictionary*, p.66

were astounded and highly alarmed by it. The same forces which successfully prevented the first exchange plan were up again to oppose the new move. Sir Samuel Forster's father was among concerned patriots who wrote petitions to the Colonial office in London denouncing the move; they argued that an exchange would hamper trade and also dilute the identity of the population. Again, their voices were heard and the move was abandoned.

Internally, this was a period of intense rivalry and hostility between the African population of Bathurst, mainly Liberated Africans and Wollof artisans; and the European merchants. The Europeans who dominated trade and the Government wanted to retain complete monopoly of the running of the Colony; the Africans however, wanted a say in commerce and the administration and were clamouring for constitutional change which would give them some influence. The demand for political representation however, was not met until 1896, when Samuel

Forster was nominated into the Legislative Council. Sir Samuel therefore grew up in a Bathurst society in flux; with his father among the rising generation of Africans slowly but steadily gaining political consciousness and aspiring for more rights including better educational facilities.

Indeed, it was for want of a high school in Bathurst that in 1885, Sir Samuel was moved to Freetown, Sierra Leone to attend the Freetown Grammar School where he remained until 1888 when he returned home to prepare to go to England for his studies. He entered Oxford University in 1893 to study Law, and in 1897 graduated with distinction. In 1898, he was called to the Bar at the prestigious Inner Temple and returned home the following year to become Gambia's first indigenous lawyer[28].

His practice attracted numerous clients from Africans in Bathurst and upriver. Many chiefs who fell foul of the colonial government and risked

---

[28] For a full obituary of Sir Samuel Forster, see Theo B Jones's tribute in *Gambia Echo* July 15, 1940, p.5

banishment or imprisonment turned to him for legal advice and support. Thus he saved many Gambian notables from the strong arms of the colonial regime. In 1901, Government asked him to accede to the post of Colonial Registrar, and in 1905 he added Commissioner of Census to his increasing portfolio. He later served as Coroner, Justice of the Peace, and Police Magistrate.

Despite numerous attempts to lure him to Nigeria where he stood to earn more money from his practice, Sir Samuel stood his ground and always said 'Under whatever circumstances, my country first'. Such was his patriotic zeal.

In early 1902, he dabbled in journalism; he accompanied the Aglo-French joint force which attacked jihadist and resistance leader Foday Kabba in Kiang, as a correspondent for the reputable Reuters news agency. His dispatches from the trenches kept the British newspapers well supplied with the progress of this war in colonial Gambia.

In 1904, he entered the Legislative Council as a Temporary Member, temporary due to his father's illness ; and when his father died in 1906, Sir Samuel was nominated permanently to the post which he held till his death in 1940. He had a brilliant, but controversial political career which requires close study.

Sir Samuel used his long stint in the Legislative Council to defend the interest of ordinary Gambians; for example, in the 1930s when motor cars were being introduced in the country, he lamented in legislative sessions, the bad state of the roads in the Protectorate that caused numerous accidents and delay in transporting trade goods. He worked, together with other Gambian legislators such as Sheikh Omar Faye and Davidson Carrol, in opposing the disbandment in 1935 of the Local Volunteer Force which engaged dozens of young Gambians who were rendered jobless following its dissolution. In 1920, he joined other nationalists, like E.F Small, to form the

Gambia Chapter of the National Council for British West Africa (NCBWA); the first nationalist movement in English speaking West Africa. He led the movement for a few years before he resigned - apparently alarmed by its increasing radical stance against colonial rule. Critics point out that Sir Samuel was too close to the colonial rulers and maybe was even antagonistic towards the calls for the franchise and self-determination. His critics also point out that he worked against the progressive social and political agenda of E.F Small. For example, he strongly supported the 1933 Licensing Ordinance and Trade Union Registration Ordinance. It was this ordinance which greatly affected Small. Small was forced to close his newspaper company for 18 months before he was able to fulfil the registration conditions of the ordinance and in 1934 lost his leadership of the Bathurst Trade Union due to technicalities in the new Ordinances.

While it is true that Sir Samuel became more accommodating of the colonial government as the years dragged on, he remained a stout defender of his people's rights. When he thought that by negotiating over issues he would win concessions for Gambians, he did so and the outcome was always beneficial to The Gambia. His experience and exposure to the workings of the colonial machinery had made him more of a pragmatic realist than an irrational political hothead. To the colonial government, he was a stabilizing phenomenon who could win them goodwill from among his people, who in turn respected him greatly for his sagacity and selflessness. In recognition of this, Samuel became Sir Samuel when he was knighted in 1933, becoming the first Gambian to be so honoured by the Colonial administration.[29]

Sir Samuel was a sociable man. He founded the Scout movement in The Gambia and was its treasurer for four decades; in 1911, he founded the Bathurst Reform Club which still exists today as a

[29] The only other Gambians to be so honoured with knighthood were: Sir John Mahoney, Sir Dawda Jawara, Sir Farimang Singhateh and Sir Alieu S Jack.

gathering for Gambian professionals most of whom were excluded from the predominantly European Clubs in Bathurst such as the European Sports Club. As a deeply religious man, he belonged to numerous Committees of the Wesleyan Church and in 1913, represented his church at the Centenary Celebrations in London of the Wesleyan Methodist Missionary Society. His marriage in 1909 produced six children all of whom outlived him.

His death on July 1940 was an occasion of great mourning in the Gambia. His colleagues in the Legislative Council such as Sheikh Omar Faye and Davidson Carrol, Governor Southern and Chief Justice Gray among others, paid tribute to him as a selfless patriot who put country before self and as a stout defender of the defenceless and of the political rights of his people.

John Andrew N'Jai -Gomez (1875-1945): Civil Servant and Social Commentator

"An Illustrious and loyal citizen, energetic and conscientious worker for the social, political and intellectual advances of his country"[30] said the *Gambia Echo* in the 1930's, a column in tribute to J.A N'Jai-Gomez after he had retired from government service. While the columnist may be excused for taking out such fulsome praises on a friend, he was not exaggerating because Njai-Gomez was indeed an outstanding personality who left his indelible mark in the political, social, and economic landscape of his country from the 1890s to his death in the early 1940s. His fruitful career was stationed on a solid educational background,

[30] See 'Pen Portrait' *Gambia Echo*, April 18, 1938, p.3. In this fulsome write up, a leading Bathurst writer D. David Jones profiles the civil achievements of Njai Gomez.

strong religious upbringing, and fervent patriotism.

Born in Bathurst in 1875, N'Jai -Gomez attended the Roman Catholic School and later the Methodist School at Hill Street. When the latter was closed in 1890 due to lack of funding, N'jai -Gomez transferred to the Dobson Street Methodist School under the legendary head teacher Victor Harding. At the time, it was common practice for boys to be engaged in learning some kind of skills or trade while still going to school, and N'jai-Gomez was no exception. This practice was influenced by the fact that at the time the leading Africans in Bathurst were the tradesmen and merchants; two occupations which attracted lucrative remuneration and high status in the society. Moreover, as most of the predominantly Muslim population did not send their children to the Christian Mission schools, children were sent to learn trades under the tutelage of great trade-masters who headed professional societies like the

Plumbers Society, Shipwright Society and the Carpenter's Society, amongst others.

N'jai-Gomez was apprenticed for ten years under Momdou Marie Njie, a well-known Bathurst carpenter and Muslim Elder, who founded and led the Carpenter's Society. Under him, the society undertook the first major renovation of the main Bathurst Mosque along Clifton Road in the 1880s.

N'jai- Gomez's links with this Muslim tradesman helped him to acquire skills and also imbued him with tolerance and open mindedness towards Muslims which he would employ to good use in later years as a mediator in the internecine intra-Muslim dissensions of the 1920s.

In 1895, N'jai-Gomez entered the Government Civil Service as a Customs Clerk and by dint of hard work and dedication to duty, he earned promotions in 1897 and 1898. Indeed, he was on the cusp of a rewarding career when he suddenly resigned from the Government Service to take up appointment in one of the leading European mercantile firms, the Bathurst Trading Company (BTC).

The BTC deserves attention because it was the oldest European firms in the Gambia. Established in 1860 as the River Gambia Trading Company, it had numerous retail stores in Bathurst and the river side towns in the interior. It had monopoly over the trade in groundnuts and bee wax; in 1907, it bought 14,000 tons of the crops in over one hundred upriver depots. This was evacuated to its warehouses in Bathurst by a fleet of twelve river vessels.

Why he resigned from the civil service remains a mystery; was he driven by youthful over ambition or pecuniary ambitions? The answer is still not clear. What is clear, however, is that he did immediately recognised that he was not cut out for work with the mercantile firm and left in 1900 to re-enter the Civil Service, where he stayed for the next twenty years.

His second stint in the civil service was eventful not only because of his numerous promotions and movements, but by his militant stance on winning better working conditions for African junior civil servants. In 1912, he spearheaded a petition to Government by civil servants for the grading of the pay scale of civil servants in The Gambia in line with the pay scale for Africans in the sister colonies of Ghana, Sierra Leone and Nigeria. Before then, Gambian clerks were paid less than their peers in the other British West African colonies. The 1912 action ended this discriminatory practice and gave Gambian civil servants better working conditions. Later in the 1930s, he also championed the rights of the over 200 African 3rd Grade Clerks in the government service who could go without promotion for twenty years because of an 'impassable barrier' created by the colonial authorities, which caused them untold penury and frustration.

Following his retirement in 1920, N'jai- Gomez's services to his people became more solid and constant; he was in the forefront of every imaginable good cause in the country ranging from improvements in girls' education, protecting the rights of Gambian seafarers, better drainage for Bathurst and campaigning for elective political representation.

He was an engaged nationalist. In 1928, he founded the Gambia Representative Committee (GRC), a gathering of patriots determined to win an elective concession from the colonial authorities[31]. Together with members like Sir Samuel Forster, Njai-Gomez won a major constitutional victory when in 1930, the Bathurst Urban District Council (BUDC) was established comprising of elected African members. This was the modest beginnings of elective politics in the Gambia. Njai-Gomez served in the BUDC from 1930-1934 and is remembered for winning better accommodation facilities for

[31] See Hughes and Perfect. *A Political History*, p.100, 101 for a detailed account of the rise of the GRC and Njai-Gomez's role in its affairs.

African patients at the Victoria Hospital in Bathurst and the liberty of civil servants to retain the services of private doctors. It was through his effort as councillor that people from the Protectorate who died in Bathurst were allowed burial rites in the town instead of transferring their bodies to the villages for internment. The Committee was also a training ground for future leaders in the Bathurst community as subsequent members of the BUDC and its unpopular successor, the Bathurst Advisory Town Council (BATC), caught their political teeth in the confines of the Committee.

He worked towards the promotion of girls' education in Bathurst. In 1920, the Methodist Girls' High School was closed after the departure of its only teacher to England. Much of the credit for the re-opening of the MGHS goes to Njai-Gomez, who, in 1920, discussed the subject with Rev. Toye, the Methodist Chaplain, in order to afford Gambian women secondary education at home. Njai-Gomez worked tirelessly to see the school start normal classes again. He recalled his daughter Ruth Njai-

Gomez, who was a senior teacher at the Girls' High School in Freetown, Sierra Leone, to come as a volunteer teacher in Banjul. She returned and became the first teacher of the re-opened MGHS in 1922. Weeks later, Njai-Gomez hired Miss Malake Auber and Chris Roberts to be assistant teachers at the school and convinced Rebecca Savage, who was a famous teacher at Dobson Street School, to become matron of the school. He raised two thousand pounds to purchase and refurbish the school building, and to ensure the survival of the school.

Njai-Gomez, in 1924, established a non-denominational Guarantors' Board for the school, which advised the master on administrative issues. But what motivated a man like him to give so much support to girls' education? First, he had successfully educated his daughters and was himself a teacher of good repute at several Bathurst schools. Second, Njai-Gomez was above all a patriot, who believed in the potentials of educated men and women to change society for the better.

He was equally concerned with the welfare of Bathurst residents which is why he vehemently opposed the plans to reclaim the town at an extortionate five thousand pounds to be paid for by Gambian taxpayers in the 1940s[32]. Instead, he stated in petitions published in the local press that Bathurst needed proper drainage systems and good sanitary measures to save it from flooding and malarial water logging. He equally campaigned against the introduction of Income Tax in 1939 to raise funds for the British war effort, arguing that it would hurt few working Gambians and serve as a deterrence to the assistance given by the wage earners to the poor and dependents.

In a series of 1937 press articles decrying the sorry state of infrastructure in Bathurst, Njai- Gomez wrote: "Any money spent on improving infrastructure for the health, prosperity and education of the people is money well spent and

---

[32] See *Gambia Echo*, 19 March 1937.

rightly spent".[33] Such was his patriotic fervour. He died in 1945 and the obituaries on him were full of praise for his selfless service to his community.

[33] Gambia Echo, 19 March 1937,

Maryann Gabbidon (1870-1938): Merchant

Maryann Gabbidon was a leading merchant in Bathurst for over forty years who sponsored her son Dr S.H.O Jones through medical studies in the UK to become The Gambia's first Director of Medical Services during the last two decades of colonial rule.[34] Denied political control by the colonialists, their agents and the chiefs; women largely resorted to commerce to become independent providers. Therefore, in the early 1900s, Banjul women became major merchants competing with European firms for control of the lucrative retail trade in consumer goods. They were inspired by precursor Mullato women merchants like Elizabeth Tigh, Mrs. Riley and Fenda

[34] See Ceesay, H. "Gabbidon, Maryann." *African American Studies Center*, edited by Ed. . *Oxford AfricanAmerican Studies Center*, http://www.oxfordaasc.com/article/opr/t356/e0053 (accessed Fri Feb 14 14:27:49 EST 2014).

Lawrence. We should pause for a moment here and dilate briefly on the contributions of these early women traders to the social and economic development of the River Gambia area in the 18th and early 19th centuries. They traded mainly in slaves and upon the demise of this baleful commerce following abolition in 1807, they were smart enough to diversify into legitimate trade dealing in wax, cloth, guns, tobacco and irons with European merchants, mainly British and French, who had trading factories in Albreda, Juffure and Bintang. Besides, the mullato women were also ladies of social import whose intermingling with Europeans along centres on the River Gambia helped to create a cosmopolitan and eclectic society in these riverside settlements.

The decline in slave dealing and the stiff competition posed by the European firms backed by their home governments brought gloom to the Mullato women traders such that they faded into oblivion. The once flamboyant and classy women were now deep in the arms of heavy drinking and immorality by the end of the 1840s.

Meanwhile, the Aku women rose to prominence in the Bathurst retail trade. Hannah Forster opened shops in several towns in the country trading in palm oil, kola nuts, oysters, groundnuts and cloth; Lucretia St. Claire Joof was a timber merchant. In the 1920s, women traders began to dominate the vegetable and fruit retail trade at the main Albert Market in Banjul, built in 1854. Kola nut dealers like Martha Thorpe were rich enough to purchase land in Banjul and develop it for their own use in the 1870s. Another market woman, Marriane Isidore, in 1882, hired Banjul lawyers to help her recover goods worth one thousand pounds owed to her by trader Barra Chow. Ya Ada Beigh was wealthy enough to hire lawyers to take her inheritance case to the Privy Council in 1929.

Indeed Banjul women were making enough money to embark on pilgrimages to Mecca or Rome and to organise expensive wedding parties even at the height of the recession in the late 1930s.

Maryann Gabbidon was therefore in a good league, and she used her wealth to subsidize her child's expensive medical studies in the UK in the 1920s and thus added another professional man to the small but progressive and highly dutiful community in Bathurst.

From humble beginnings selling cooked food in the Bathurst Albert market in the 1890s, Maryann soon saved enough money to import kola nuts from Portuguese Guinea and Sierra Leone. By 1911, she was the importer of this popular stimulant in the Gambia. She established shops in the major riverside towns such as Bintang, Kauntaur and Fatoto, and was highly respected in the Protectorate by her customers and competitors. Competition was offered by the European firms and other African merchants like the Carrols and S.H Jones, who also figured prominently in the retail trade up river at the turn of the 19th century.[35]

---

[35] See Ceesay, H. Gambian Women: Profiles and Historical Notes, Fulladu Publishers, 2010, p.11.

In the 1930s, the government in French Senegal made kola nuts a non-dutiable commodity, and this brought unfair competition and great loses to kola nut merchants like Maryann. She avoided closing shop by diversifying her business into selling cotton goods and other types of linen in the protectorate.

Maryann was a successful mother who bore four children who all received foreign education in Sierra Leone and England to become notable professionals[36]. Most notable is Dr. S.H.O Jones, born in 1910, in 1935 became one of the first Gambian surgeons, and later rose to the high rank of Director of Medical Services, and from 1972 to 1977 Speaker of the House of Representatives. Maryann spent five hundred pounds sterling between 1928-1935 paying parts of his medical school fees at University of Manchester, after the colonial authorities could not continue supporting his studies. Another son, Edwin studied accountancy in the UK and became the African

---

[36] See 'Tribute', *Gambia Echo*, 7 November 1938, p.5

Accountant at the Public Works Department (PWD) in the 1930s.

Perhaps Maryann spent generously when educating her children because she herself received a sound education in the 1880s when very few Gambian girls attended school. She attended St. Mary's school in Bathurst, and the famous Annie Walsh Secondary school in Freetown, Sierra Leone, where she ranked top of her class in the Senior Cambridge examinations. She returned home in 1888 to teach. Her parentage also may have influenced her strong business credentials. Her father Charles Benjamin was a successful groundnuts trader in the protectorate who owned several cutters plying the river during the groundnuts buying season transporting the crop from buying centres to Bathurst. This was major occupation at the last three decades of the 19th century, employing hundreds of Gambians as cutter crews, engine drivers and harbour men. Sadly, the 1936 Gambia River Navigation Law scuttled the river craft industry making many individuals redundant and broke. The law gave government river crafts like 'Lady Denham' 'Prince of Wales' priority in river transport contracts over the Gambian boat owners, and by 1940, the Half Die River side was said to be littered with hundreds of redundant boats no longer able to compete against Government fleet[37].

She epitomized the Bathurst woman of the late 19th and early 20th centuries who made up for their failure to get through the educational and administrative system by engaging in petty trading and other forms of business with all their efforts and came out wealthy, and highly respected in society. As they spent their fortunes in fineries, big houses, and lavish society weddings, they also paid for their children's education in the best schools along the coast and in England. Women like Maryann therefore were builders of talents for their country.

---

37 For a mention of this controversial Ordinance, see *Gambia Echo* 5 July 1937, p.5

Her success in commerce also points out to the little understood role of the River Gambia in the economic and political empowerment of Gambians. While it is true that the River Gambia enticed Europeans into the country because of its trade potentials, it also enabled local Gambians like Maryann to build success in trading which gave them the wherewithal to educate their children who would later lead the nationalist struggle for independence. Such commercial success also translated into financial support to the early nationalist political parties.

Upon her death in November 1938, an obituary in the respected Gambia Echo said of her "by dint of hardwork, courage and perseverance she succeeded in giving her children good education which equipped them for life's challenges'.[38]

---

[38] See Tribute," *Gambia Echo* (Bathurst), 7 November 1938.

Alhaji Ousman Jeng (1878-1960): Political Leader, Merchant and Muslim Elder

Alhaji Ousman Jeng was the leading Muslim elder, trader, politician and administrator in Bathurst in the 1920s and 30s. As one of the first Muslims to receive western education in a Mission school, he was the natural choice when Governor Armitage decided in 1922 to have a Muslim representative among the African members of the Legislative Council, and he served two terms up to 1932 when he was replaced on the Council by Sheikh Omar Faye. He ably represented the Bathurst Muslim Community, and was seen as a moderate voice in the Council trusted by successive colonial Governors who sat as Chairmen of the Council.

Jeng however, had cut his political teeth in the Gambia chapter of the highly nationalistic and radically anti-colonial National Council for British West Africa (NCBWA) led by E.F Small. Jeng was among the first Muslims to join the NCBWA Gambia section, and was soon appointed leader of its Muslim Wing[39]. In 1921, he suddenly resigned accusing the NCBWA Gambia Section of 'inability to deliver the goods'; he immediately fell into the favour of Governor Armitage, a vehement opponent of Small and the NCBWA, who nominated him first Muslim member of the legislature. This appointment served the other purpose of creating dissension in the NCBWA Gambia Section's Muslim supporters, who were now caught between following their political leader out of the group, or staying put; many opted out, and this cost the NCBWA a large chunk of its Muslim members. Jeng worked against the NCBWA, and in numerous letters to Governor Armitage denounced the association as 'poisonous'; with the support of Bathurst Imam Omar Sowe, an ally of his, he sidelined pro-

[39] See Hughes and Perfect (2006) p.91, 100.

congress Muslims like Sheikh Omar Faye in Government activities.

This greatly distressed the Bathurst Muslims such that in 1929, it spilt on to the pulpit of the main Mosque when supporters of Faye prevented the Imam from doing his sermons in protest over his links with Jeng. The mistrust between the Jeng-Faye factions also flowed into the running of the Mohammedan School created in 1903 in response to Muslim demands for a Western school friendly to their religion. Faye's faction favoured the promotion of Ousman Njie Gormack, an ally, as manager of the school, while the Jeng faction opposed the move. This led to a standoff which lasted throughout 1939, and the school was nearly closed as a result by the colonial authorities, perplexed by the situation. Indeed, from 1928 to 1935, it was the rivalry between Jeng and Faye that characterized the state of Muslims in Bathurst and it cost the community dearly in terms of trust of the colonial authorities who insisted on dealing with only a united Muslim block.

Historians like Langley, Hughes and Perfect have wondered at the reason for the unhealthy rivalry between the two Muslim elders[40]. Among the possible causes were caste and class origins, differences in view about the nature of political representation for Muslims (Jeng did not support elections while Faye's supporters favoured elections to choose the Muslim legislator), and personal religious beliefs (tarikh).To these we should add the invidious divisive role of the mercantile firms who dealt with both men who were traders of repute, and thus did not want them to mount a united front against the exploitative tendencies of these European firms. Indeed, like Faye, Jeng was in continuous debt to the Bathurst firms and this made them unable to raise any critical voice against the foreign firms, and thus curtailed some of their political rights.

---

[40] See Langley, 'The Gambia Chapter…' p.387; Hughes and Perfect, 2008.

Jeng was a shrewd politician who mended fences with opponents like E.F Small and was able to remain relevant in Bathurst politics until his last days. At the end of his second term in the legislature in 1932, he quickly repaired relations with E. F Small and joined the Rate Payers Associations (RPA), a nationalist movement formed by Small in 1929 to canvas for the franchise in Bathurst.

From 1932 to 1936, Jeng headed the RPA Bathurst New Town Branch, and in 1936 won the BATC Councillor seat for this ward under RPA support. This U-turn from moderation to radicalism was indeed spectacular; it showed that he was a realist and pragmatist who was able to read the Bathurst political temperature well. Also, by doing so he was atoning for the frustration he caused to many of his supporters when he opposed the historic 1929 Dockers Strike for better working conditions. Dockers fed up with the exploitation by the mercantile firms downed tools for two months under the leadership of EF Small asking for increased wages and job protection. He opposed the strike because of his close business ties with Palmine and UAC, two of the firms targeted by the strikers; he used this link to also mediate a successful end of the strike in November 1929 just before the start of the groundnuts buying season.

His political longevity was phenomenal. While his peers had long left active politics, Alhaji Ousman was still active; in 1952, he helped PS Njie found the United Party and nominated him for the Legislative Council elections of 1954 which PS won, kick starting a brilliant political career. In 1959, he joined much younger political activists like A.E Cham-Joof to form the Committee of Citizens to militate against the so-called Governor Wyn-Harris Constitution which brought universal adult suffrage, but failed to give a definitive date for independence.

He was involved in Bathurst religious life for over fifty years. He sat in the Bathurst Muslim Elders Committee, and in the Management Board of the

Muhamedan School from 1936-1938. In 1935, he and other Muslim elders formed an umbrella Muslim Association which reconciled the various Muslim factions of Bathurst and was elected its Chairman. He was a close disciple of the venerable Alhaji Malick Sy, the Tijaniya leader in Tivavoune, whom he represented in Bathurst.

An overview of Alhaji Ousman's life cannot be complete without a mention of his illustrious career in business. He worked with all the major mercantile firms in Bathurst such as CFAO, Maurel et Freres and Jones Coy[41] as a trader buying groundnuts in various upriver stations such as Njawara, Kosemar, Georgetown, Kaur and Salikenni. He built a solid reputation for honesty and philanthropy. However, like other Gambian traders at the time, he fell into debt to the European firms and had to wind up his business activities upriver due to bankruptcy. Not that these Gambian traders like Alhaji Ousman were reckless or

[41] Interview with AE Cham Joof, notable historian, Gambia National Museum, Banjul, 2002

incompetent, but their plight was due to the murky business tactics of the European firms. We need to look at these briefly: firstly, the firms cobbled together into a cabal called the Chamber of Commerce into which Africans, like Alhaji Ousman, could not sit as members. In the Chamber, the prices for the groundnuts crop were predetermined ; likewise the commissions to pay middlemen like Alhaji Ousman were determined. Gambian producers and agents for the firms therefore had no say in their remuneration. By 1940, the commission paid to agents fell from sixty shillings per ton to a mere ten shilling. Moreover, by 1941, agents were to buy their own buying tools like scales, shovels and empty sacks. This seriously impoverished the traders and put them into huge debts. Indeed, by the late 1940s, the newly arrived Syrians and Lebanese who now employed the Gambians as intermediaries or coaxers had replaced Gambian traders in the Protectorate.

Alhaji was born in 1878 in Bathurst and attended the Daara of Imam Omar Sowe and the Dobson school . He had three wives and many of his sons were prominent in business and politics. B.S.O Jeng was Mayor of Banjul, and Alieu (1903-1965) was a wealthy trader and political activist who served in the legislature in the 1950s and was a member of the Constitutional Review Commission which drew up the 1954 constitution. Alhaji Ousman died in Bathurst on 26 February 1960.

John Finden Dailey (1883-1955): Nationalist Journalist

John Finden Dailey was a crusading Gambian journalist whose exposure of racism at Bansang hospital in 1948 pitted him against the colonial authorities. A contest from which he emerged unscathed, and a hero among the community.

Before we delve into his interesting career as a newspaper man and local politician, we should set the stage by looking at the history and role of the newspaper in colonial Gambia from 1883 when the first newspaper was published in Bathurst to 1942 when Finden established his *Gambia Weekly News* tabloid.

Interestingly, the earliest Bathurst newspapers were all funded and owned by rich Aku merchants or European traders who wished to have an outlet to publicize their businesses and voice out their concerns as men of commerce. The *Bathurst Observer*, the earliest newspaper to circulate in the Colony in 1883 was owned by a consortium of business moguls including Thomas Chown, John Finden and G. Goddard. It folded up in 1891. In 1893, another group of prominent Aku merchants including Sam Forster, Edmund Thomas, Horton Jones and A.W Carrol teamed up to found the *Gambia Intelligencer* newspaper under the editorship of a Sierra Leone émigré Lance Taylor. He wrote his vitriolic anti-colonial columns under the pen name of Gambay Watchman. When he left for home in 1898, the paper died as the syndicate was no longer interested in its affairs. There ensued a hiatus of 25 years when no newspaper was published locally. In 1923, E.F Small established his *Gambia Outlook* newspaper, the first press house to claim complete independence from vested mercantile interest. In 1934, another syndicate comprising Sir Sam Forster, Davidson Carrol, and J.A Njai-Gomez, disturbed by Small's vociferous anti-establishment tone, joined finances to form the

Gambia Echo under the editorship of Finden Dailey and later, Lenrie Ingram Peters. In 1938, Fiden went his own way to establish his *Gambia Weekly News*[42].

The *Weekly News* soon won the hearts of readers for its fair and balanced comments on burning national issues. It was seen as the centrist paper in between the highly nationalistic tone of Small's *Outlook* and the moderately pro-establishment *Echo*. It prided itself with scoops about racist treatment of Gambian workers in government offices, and its exposures embarrassed the colonial administration into sanctioning many of its European officials. Perhaps the *Weekly News'* most celebrated case was the Dr. Samuel Gordon case of 1948. In early 1948 while he was attending the Chief's conference in Bansang, Finden had taken time off from covering the proceedings to visit the new hospital. Besides the terrible conditions of patients and workers amidst the 'tense atmosphere of unhappiness', he

[42] See V*anguard* 7 March, 1955, see also 'Tribute' *Gambia Echo*, 7 March 1955, p.6.

witnessed a shocking scene of Dr. Gordon inspecting hernia patients by parading them naked in the open to select which cases to attend. He meticulously gathered eyewitness accounts of Dr. Gordon's humiliating treatment of patients. Finden wrote the story in the March 31st issue of the paper. The colonial government charged him for publishing a false and defamatory story, and committed him to trial which aroused the interest of the entire country. After two months of trial, he was acquitted on the grounds that the story was in the public interest, and Dr. Gordon was relieved of his duties at the hospital.

Earlier, in 1941 he had been charged with contempt of court for reporting in his newspaper details about a baby dumping case in Half Die, Bathurst, while the matter was in court. What made this trial more memorable however, was the remark of the trial judge to Finden: "Consider in your interest the advisability of the continuance of your paper. The country is small and there are already two papers in the field". These words were seen by sections of the society as a veiled threat, and an attempt to muzzle the fearless editor. Finden of course did not pay heed to the threat. In 1944, he strongly opposed the press laws enacted by Governor Blood which brought about censorship of newspapers by the information office in Bathurst. On many occasions, he refused to submit his galleys to the Government censor Captain Peters for verification; instead he chose publish his paper with most of the pages empty.

It was in recognition of his editorial abilities that in 1950, his fellow local newspaper editors chose him to represent them at an international press conference organized by Whitehall to update the press on plans for constitutional development in Britain's African colonies. Finden may have been chosen also because of his practical experience in colonial politics in the 1940s as Councillor on the Bathurst Town Council where he served two terms between the years 1942-1947.

Finden was in the league of fearless and fiercely patriotic editors like Small, Theo Jones, Mustapha Colley, M.B Jones and James Senegal who used the newspaper columns to defend the interest of their people and country against vested mercantile and colonial imperial desires. They helped to establish a vibrant press culture in the Gambia that survived the harsh realities of the colonial period and contributed to the eventual rise to independence in 1965.

In 1952, however, he came under intense criticism from his readers who were disturbed by his fierce and unguarded attacks on Garba

Jahumpa's Muslim Congress Party which he called 'fanatical' and 'tom tom boys'. He was perhaps alarmed that the Congress was taking away many supporters from P.S Njie's UP which he helped form and was using his newspaper to wage a vendetta. In the same year, he again fell into controversy when he was accused of masterminding the rift between Rev. J.C Faye,

Minister without Portfolio and Governor Wyn Harris which made Faye to be sacked from the Government. Perhaps both incidents were proof of the influence that newspaper men like him wielded during the colonial period in Bathurst.

Finden was born in Bathurst 1883, and attended the Wesley Primary School, and Methodist Boys' High School before working as a clerk with various firms in Bathurst. Upon his death in February 1955, he was mourned as 'ever ready and willing to help everyone and solve every difficulty'.[43]

[43] See 'Obituary' *Gambia Echo*, February 15 1955.

Sir John Mahoney (1883-1966): First Speaker of the Gambian Legislature

The Gambia's first legislative assembly was established in 1843. It was comprised of British c olonial officers, representatives of the colony's business community and the colonial Governor who presided over legislative business. The constitutional amendments of 1951 provide for the position of a vice president of the Legislative Council (Legco) who would conduct legislative sessions in lieu of the president, the colonial Governor. The title 'Speaker' only entered the constitution in 1954 when further amendments provided for a Gambian Speaker fully responsible for the conduct of the affairs of the Legco. This pioneering and honorific responsibility fell on to the broad shoulders of Sir John Mahoney.

His career as Speaker was dotted with political milestones including the promulgation of several constitutions and the emergence of many political parties. But equally interesting was his life before his tenure as Speaker of the Legco.

Sir John Mahoney was born in Bathurst on 6th March, 1883, the son of James Emmanuel Mahoney and his wife, Priscillia. Sir John Mahoney was educated at Wesley School Bathurst and at Church Missionary Society Grammar School in Freetown, Sierra Leone. It was then the trend for middle class Gambian Akus to send their wards to Freetown to pursue secondary education which was unavailable locally and also to be fully acculturated into Aku life.

He returned to Bathurst and worked for his father, after whose death he joined civil service and served in the Receiver General's Department between 1912 and 1916. In 1916, he joined the clerical staff of Maurel et Prom, a Bathurst- based retail firm, where he worked until his retirement in 1953.

Earlier in 1931, Sir John Mahoney was made a Justice of Peace by Governor Sir Richard Palmer, KBE. Further constitutional amendments in the mid1940s provided for more Gambian representations in the Legco and Sir John Mahoney was among the official members of the council nominated by the colonial governor. He sat in the Legco from 1942 till 1954 when he became speaker, he presided over the legislature's debate on many important issues on the Gambia constitution order-in- council, promulgated in April 1950, which brought universal adult suffrage and increased the representation of chiefs in the legislature to multiparty democracy in the Gambia with the holding of the Gambia's first general elections in May 1960[44]. Also, it was in his first tenure as speaker that Gambian members of the executive council, with similarities to a cabinet, began to appear regularly before the legislative council to account for the activities and budgets of their new ministers.

---

[44] See Hughes and Perfect,(2006) p.49-50.

Furthermore, as speaker, Sir John Mahoney represented the Gambia in several international functions including the impromptu coronation ceremonies of Queen Elizabeth in 1953. In 1960, Sir John Mahoney was granted private audience with HRH the Queen who bestowed on him the knighthood of Saint James for dedicated service to the Gambia and the Empire.

Following the epochal 1960 general elections, Sir John Mahoney was unanimously re-elected speaker of the new enlarged legislature, renamed the House of Representatives. It consisted of twenty-seven members from three political parties, independents, and chiefs' representatives. Despite his advanced age, Sir John Mahoney presided over the affairs of the house with remarkable zest and inimitable impartiality. His timely and well-toned interventions during debates maintained order and decorum in the politically disparate House.

Although he did not participate in the 1961 Gambia Constitution Talks in London, as speaker he presided over the heated pre-Marlborough House debates on a common agenda for all the participants to the talks. Unfortunately, this fell through and all the political parties proceeded to London with different agendas.

On the eve of his retirement in 1962, he again had the onerous duty to preside over the house debates on another constitution which provided for a deputy speaker and increased the house to thirty two members.

Prior to his entry into local politics, Sir John Mahoney had actively participated in the affairs of the National Council of British West Africa (NCBWA), the pioneer nationalist movement composed of West African patriots like E. F Small, Nigeria's Herbert Macaulay, S.H. M. Jones of the Gambia and Nnamdi Azikive of Nigeria. They called for more freedom for the West African colonies and condemned taxation without representation. Sir John Mahoney was a founder member of the NCBWA, Bathurst chapter[45]; he with his brother- in- law E. F. Small and other Gambian activists successfully organized the 1926 Bathurst congress of the nationalist movement despite the incessant slander and contempt heaped on their selves by the colonial authorities. Sir John Mahoney's deep interest in the NCBWA encouraged his election as secretary general of its Bathurst chapter by the five hundred local NCBWA memberships. Indeed, his great mobilizing skills and spell-binding oratory won him the respect of other NCBWA local heavyweights like H. M. Jones, Ousman Jeng, and E.F Small who shared his nationalist dispositions.

Besides his political activism, Sir John Mahoney also served in many important positions of responsibility in the church and government. He served in the Gambia education committee, on the Elliot commission for Higher Education in West

[45] See Langley, J. A Africa, 1969, 'The Gambia Chapter of the National Council of British West Africa p.382.

Africa, set up in the mid-1940s to draw a blueprint for colonial education development in West Africa. A staunch Methodist, he represented the Gambia at many church conferences in West Africa and beyond.

Sir John was also a dedicated family man. He married early and was blessed with two sons, three daughters and several grandchildren. Among his daughters was Lady Augustus Mahoney, consort of Sir D.K. Jawara, who was the first woman parliamentary candidate in Gambia and simultaneously a playwright, nurse, and social worker. Sir John's wife, Lady Mahoney, was a devout church woman and Aku socialite who became a fountain of strength and inspiration for Sir John, whose health was never robust.

Sir John Mahoney died in February 1966. He will be remembered as the Gambia's first speaker; who presided over the adoption of four constitutions by the legislature, one of which saw the Gambia through to independence; a staunch NCBWA activist and nationalist; a devout Methodist, and a successful family man.

Alhaji Sheikh Omar Faye (1889-1959): Muslim Missionary, Trader and Politician

'He was a most popular and most dynamic figure in Gambian politics, where for over 19 years he creditably retained his seat in the Legislative Council. He was The Gambia's representative in May 1937 at the coronation of King George VI. He was an erudite Quranic scholar who went to Mecca on several occasions, a great international figure in the Muslim world, and a staunch believer in the universal brotherhood of men in Allah', thus ran a tribute to Alhaji Sheikh Omar Fye when he died in 1959.[46]

Born in Banjul in 1889, pursued Quranic studies, and attended Wesley School until 1903. From 1903 to 1904, he studied at the newly founded

[46] See *Vanguard*, Bathurst, 1959, p.2

Muhammedan school cutting short his studies in 1906, after the death of his father, to start work.

He began his working life as a clerk at Georgetown for the United African Company (UAC) before leaving to work with a Syrian trader posted at Njawara where he married his first wife[47]. Although working, he continued to quench his thirst for Islamic knowledge and jurisprudence. During the off groundnuts trade season, when business activity was dull, he would travel to Senegal to study under great scholars such as Alhaji Abdoulie Niasse, founder of Niassen brotherhood in Kaolack, Senegal, and the famous Bathurst Imam, teacher and Cadi, Waka Bah. He was in close contact with Alhaji Malick Sy of Tivavoune, Sheikh Ahmad Bamba of Touba, the founder of the Mouride and Seydina Tall. At Njawara, he organized an annual Muslim gathering which attracted hundreds of

---

[47] See 'A great Gambian Scholar...' *Daily Observer*, 17 December 1993. See also, *Gambia Echo* January 8, 1940. See also Hughes and Perfect (2006) p.111, 119 for a more detail account of the career of Mr Faye.

worshippers from Senegal and Gambia, and as the size of his disciples increased, he established a cleric village called Sanchi Sheikh Fye.

He was treading in the footsteps of his mentors like Mam Bamba and Abdoulie Niasse who also established religious settlements to be away from the hustle and bustle of the towns and dedicated himself to religious worship and comprehension. He built a mosque and a big shed to accommodate his talibes.[48] When he returned to Bathurst in 1927, the village was deserted and his disciples followed him to the town. His children were sent to prestigious religious schools in Kaolack and Piir in Senegal, while others attended the Muhamedan School in Bathurst; he put value in both religious and secular education. After a hiatus of fifteen years when he was deeply involved in nationalist politics, Sheikh Omar returned to religious missionary work in 1952 when he toured West Africa on his way to perform the Hajj, preaching and converting many people in Kono, Sierra Leone

---

[48] The Wollof word for Quranic pupil.

and Northern Ghana. Armed with a letter of introduction from Governor Sir Percy Wyn Harris, Sheikh Omar toured northern Nigeria where he was warmly welcomed by the Emir of Kano and the Sultan of Sokoto, the spiritual leader of Nigerian Muslims. In Nigeria and Chad, he helped to settle land and chieftaincy disputes which had bewildered the colonial authorities. When he reached Saudi Arabia in 1953, he was feted by Crown Prince Ibn Saud whom he had met in London in 1937 during the Coronation, and was guest of the Saudi royals for five months.

He returned to The Gambia briefly in 1954. The following year, he embarked on another pilgrimage and missionary trip which lasted three years. In Kono, Sierra Leone he converted hundreds and built schools and a mosque. In Ghana, Sheikh Omar served as election observer in the crucial Gold Coast elections of 1956, and his certification of the election, convinced Governor Clarke to cede nationhood to Ghana.

This was the denouement of his involvement in politics which started in 1932 when he was nominated into the Legislative Council to replace Ousman Jeng as Muslim member of the legislative body.

Until he lost his Legco seat to E.F Small in 1947, Sheikh Omar was the most important political figure in the Gambia. He was trusted by his people and the colonial government, a rare accolade at the time as not many public figures were able to manoeuvre the dilemma of serving in colonial establishments, like the Legco, whilst also being sensitive to the plight of the local people. He was assisted by his tact, intelligence and honesty. Together, with other Legislators like Sir Samuel Forster and Davidson Carrol, he embodied the aspirations of Gambians by always enquiring about the welfare of the people at the Legislature meetings. For example, he championed better medical facilities for Bansang hospital to serve the Protectorate and frequently asked questions related to the development of agriculture in the provinces[49]. He was an astute farmer who owned a big farm at Makka Bala Manneh in Niumi where he experimented with the growing of shea butter trees[50]. In 1940, when there was disquiet in the farming community over the poor producer price for groundnuts, Governor Southern sent Sheikh Omar on a charm offensive to explain to farmers that plans were afoot to increase price.

As a matter of fact, he was a successful businessman who imported cattle from Mauritania, opened the first indigenous car marketing firm in Bathurst which sold British brands like Vanguard, and also was a major groundnuts dealer. He was among the few Gambians who resisted the dominance of foreign firms and Syrians in retail trade by pursuing their own successful businesses. However, as such, Gambian traders were still dependent on the Syrians and European firms for transportation and loans, unsuccessful trade

---

[49] For more details on his Legco contributions, see *Gambia Echo,* 5 February 1940.
[50] See CSO 3/87, Gambia National Archives; see also CSO 3/144, Gambia National Archives, Banjul.

seasons could mean big losses and high debts which forced many of them to close business. Ill health and mounting debts forced him to close his shops in 1954.

He died in 1959 and was mourned widely in the Gambia and abroad.

Hannah Forster (1893-1966): Merchant and Political Leader

Hannah Forster was born on 14 January 1893 in Banjul to Elizabeth Johnson, and Mr C. C. Johnson, an Aku civil servant, who was among the educated men sent down from Freetown to occupy senior civil service jobs in The Gambia.[51] Hannah was an accomplished woman politician, merchant, seamstress, church worker and social activist. A pioneer in many spheres, she was the first woman to sit on the Bathurst Town Council in the early 1930s; this made her the first Gambian woman to go into active politics.[1]

In 1893, The Gambia was struggling to survive as a separate colony after it was excised from Sierra

[51] See Ceesay, H. 'Hannah Forster'. *Dictionary of African Biography*, Emmanuel K Akyeampong and Henry Louis Gates Jr. (eds), Oxford University Press, 2012; see also Ceesay, H. *Gambian Women: An Introductory History*, Banjul, Gambia, Fulladu Publishers, 2008.

Leone in 1887. Educational opportunities were limited to St Mary's Primary and Wesley Preparatory in Banjul; secondary education was available only in Freetown. With limited educational opportunities, very few indigenous Gambians occupied any position in the civil service. The Colony depended on the British colonies along the coast for educated labour and professionals such as clerks, printers and teachers. Slave raiding fuelled the insecurity in the hinterland, which was still out of British jurisdiction, in the control of local rulers like Musa Molloh, the King of Fulladu, and Foday Kaba Dumbuya, the overlord of Kiang or Foday Sillah, the Imam of Kombo.

Forster, therefore, grew up in the shifting political economy of the colonial period when opportunities for self-actualization, especially for women, were a distant dream, which very few Gambians achieved. However, a combination of caring parenthood and a persistent determination to succeed motivated her to overcome the odds stacked against her and many of her peers in The Gambia at the dawn of the 20th century. After her primary education at St Mary's Elementary School in Banjul, she proceeded to Freetown for her secondary schooling. A sad development in her family forced her to cut her studies short, but being a brilliant student she had been able to get enough education to become a junior teacher at her former school in Banjul. Whilst teaching, she continued to hone her sewing skills and left her classroom job to venture into self-employment. She started a retail business and ran a sewing workshop. This decision was in itself quite courageous at the time. Regular paid employment was so hard to come by that it was unheard of for anyone who got it to leave it for something less certain.

Forster was driven by her strong belief in economic independence for women, and also the wish to learn enough to educate her children and take care of her dependants. When her husband died so early in their marriage, leaving her with two children, she became more determined to do well in her business. She expanded it into the protectorate, and set up a retail and tailoring shop at the coastal town of Kartong. Unlike other Banjul merchants who traded in the hinterland only during the four months of the groundnut trade season, Hannah's Kartong shop operated all year round, which won her the respect of the community. By the late 1930s, her success in business had put her in good stead to start the import/export trade in kola nuts and oysters between Banjul and the UK, Freetown and Lagos. She supplied kola nuts to traders in protectorate centres such as Kaur, Kuntaur and Nianimaro, and exported oysters to Lagos and Liverpool. She opened the first fashion shop in Banjul that sold her own sewing and designer labels from Europe. She was in the league of other industrious women traders such as Mammy Gabbidon and Mammy Monday, who were also importers of luxury goods for the Banjul elite. Forster owned several properties in Banjul and the Kombos. When her father was ageing in Freetown, he asked her to run his vast trade concerns there; such was the confidence she had built in business circles.

She was able to earn enough money to educate her children and to become a major political figure in Banjul. Her daughter Catherine Collier studied in the UK, became the first Gambian radiographer in September 1954 and, in 1957, a visiting journalist described her as 'one of the few women in Banjul who are able to combine a career with being a mother'. Her son, Dr Bani Forster, became the first African qualified psychiatrist and later worked in Ghana.[2]

Forster became the first Gambian woman to take part in militant politics in the 1930s when she sat as an elected councillor on the Banjul Town Advisory Council, later the Banjul Town Council. She excelled in council debates and activities and retained her seat in several elections. The council collected taxes and rates to finance minor development schemes such as parks, markets and roads. Upon the completion of her final term as

Councillor in 1952, a supporter commented thus: 'Though of the female gender, Mrs. Forster was always masculine in the expression of her views in the Council which enabled her to keep pace with men both intellectually and philosophically. She is a woman of integrity who will be hard to replace'[52].

In 1951, she joined the Rev. J. C. Faye to form The Gambia's first political party, the Gambia Democratic Party (GDP).[53] This put her in the middle of Banjul nationalist politics. She founded the Women's Wing of the party, and became its leading *yai compin* and financier. She co-authored the GDP's manifesto published in preparation for the crucial first party- based elections in The Gambia in October 1954. On her insistence, the Manifesto called for 'developing trade with other British West African territories' and for a 'freer border trade' with Senegal, a reflection of her strong feelings about the importance of trade in national development. The success of the GDP

[52] See *Gambia Echo* 18 February 1952, p.12.
[53] See, Ceesay, H. 'Hannah Forster', p.384, Oxford University Press.

candidate, J C Faye, in the elections and his subsequent appointment as one of the first three Gambian ministers in November 1954 owe much to Forster's mobilization capabilities, financing and popular touch.

She used her wealth to support many GDP activities especially during the 1960 election campaign in which the party fielded candidates in all the seven colony constituencies. Of even greater significance is the critical role Forster played in the January 1959 All-Party Conference held at Jangjangbureh at which political leaders and chiefs met to discuss crucial issues about The Gambia's political evolution. As one of the very few women present at the meeting, she supported the Rev. J. C. Faye's stand that protectorate women should be given the vote in any future constitution. Her persistent tenacity combined with Faye's highly passionate arguments convinced the reluctant chiefs to agree on enfranchising women at a conference held at Brikama in February, 1959.

Much earlier, Forster served on the consultative committee appointed by Governor Sir Percy Wynn Harris in 1953 to draw up a framework for a new constitution for The Gambia. The Committee met in different parts of the country between May 1953 and January 1954 to sound popular opinion on the future constitution. The Committee made drastic constitutional proposals such as the appointment of a speaker for the Legislative Council, which was to be enlarged to 16 members, appointment of Gambian ministers, and holding party-based elections in the colony. Forster was given the honour of presenting the report of the committee to the visiting Secretary of State for the Colonies, Oliver Lytleton. The proposals were accepted and formed the basis of the 1954 Constitution.[3]

Forster was also an active church worker. She served on many voluntary bodies of the Anglican Diocese, and worked hard to bring women to the forefront of church activities in Banjul. She founded the Mothers' Union, a philanthropic organization that built a day-care nursery at Banjulding to cater for working mothers. She was truly a woman of unparalleled dexterity and courage, who qualifies to be in the league of great Gambian women.

Matarr Ceesay (1890-1971): Traditional Leader and Farmer

Upper Saloum District in the Central River Region was created in 1902 as District No. 5 by the Colonial authorities under the Protectorate Ordinance of 1893. It covers an area of 88 square miles. The District was under the Kingdom of Pakala ruled by powerful kings such as Gedel Mbodge, Biram Sisay and Sawallo Ceesay. Sawallo , was re-appointed by the British as Chief of the new district in 1893 by Traveling Commissioner Ozanne. Sawallo was replaced as Chief in 1919 by his son Omar, who was replaced in 1933 by Laein Dado. In 1935, Matarr Ceesay, youngest son of Sawallo, was appointed chief.

He was among the few educated chiefs, having attended the Muhameddan School in the 1910s, before working as interpreter for the Traveling

Commissioner, North Bank Province.[54] Interpreters were central to the running of the colonial machinery as they were the intermediaries between the local people and the Colonial officials. They were sometimes feared for they could cause grief to anyone they did not like by misrepresenting their views to the British officials. Also, they wielded influence because of their perceived proximity to the colonial powers; the European officials also did not always trust the interpreters and occasionally would have them sacked or jailed for suspected treachery.

Being educated, Chief Matarr 'encouraged the building of schools in his district'; in 1947 schools were opened at Njau and Kaur. He coaxed village Alkalis to send their eldest male children to the schools so that the majority of the first corps of

---

[54] See Ceesay, H. "Ceesay, Matarr." *African American Studies Center*, edited by Ed. . *Oxford AfricanAmerican Studies Center*, http://www.oxfordaasc.com/article/opr/t356/e0053 (accessed Fri Feb 14 14:27:49 EST 2014).

educated people from the district were sons of Alkalis.[55]

In April 1952, he organized in Upper Saloum the first ever Cattle Market in The Gambia in which a large number of animals were on view and butchers travelled from all parts of the country to buy livestock[56]. He did this to reduce the price hike of livestock by Senegalese and Mauritanian dealers and also to reduce the overgrown herds in the district and other parts of the country. He continued to organise the cattle fair until his death and it has remained an annual national event since then. To promote agriculture in Upper Saloum, Chief Matarr started a campaign of growing citrus plants in the district, and introduced benni (sesame) seeds in the region. The rest house he built at Njau for the comfort of the Traveling Commissioners was the best in the provinces, and in the 1957 Report on Chiefs, it was related that

---

[55] See 'Ceesay, Matarr' in Ceesay, H. Oxford African American Studies Centre.
[56] See *Gambia Echo*, 5 May 1952, p.10.

Chief Matarr had industriously built causeways, wharves and bridges at Panchang, Nioro and Sam.

From 1947-1954, he sat as one of the Chiefs' representatives in the Legislative Council. Mama Tamba Jammeh and Karamo Sanneh were the other chiefs in the Legco. Chief Matarr's performance at the Legco was exemplary: he advocated for better producer prices for groundnuts and frequently attacked the profiteering tactics of the Syrian and Lebanese traders in the Protectorate. When the PPP was formed in 1959, he and Mama Tamba were among the first chiefs to lend their support to the new party. Chief Matarr's son, Omar contested the Saloum seat on the PPP ticket in 1960. Yet, there were other commonalities that the two famous chiefs, Matarr and Mama Tamba shared: both men attended Muhammedan School in Bathurst and their literacy enabled them to plan and execute small scale infrastructure developments such as wharves, causeways and roads. Furthermore, Chief Mama Tamba and Chief Matarr played key roles in the Legislature between 1947 and 1954 representing the interest of the Protectorate peoples in the law making body. In 1948, they represented The Gambia at the British West Africa Chiefs' Conference in London which brought together traditional rulers from all over West Africa.

Chief Matarr died in September 1961.

Edward Francis Small (1890-1958): Crusading Journalist and Nationalist Politician

David Perfect, a leading scholar on Gambian labour history gave this very succinct introduction to the life times of E.F Small:

> Small's achievements include being the founder of the Gambia branch of the National Council British West Africa (NCBWA), the first inter-territorial political organization of the region; the first Gambian to be directly elected to the Legislative Council and the first to be appointed to the Executive Council (cabinet). He was also the most important leader of the Bathurst Rate Payers Association, which dominated municipal politics in Bathurst in the 1930s and 1940s;

> founded the first Gambian trade union; established a cooperative movement for farmers and created the modern Gambian press.[57]

Mr. Small was a nationalist politician, trade unionist, journalist and crusader for social justice who spent his entire life striving for freedom and justice for his people. Unfortunately, he died before seeing the seeds of sovereignty he helped sow germinate to full independence for The Gambia. Small's father, a teacher, sent him to school at the age of five and at 15 he went to Freetown to pursue High School education.

In 1911, he joined the Sierra Leone civil service as trainee clerk. He returned home in 1914, and became interested in trade unionism and began to organize civil servants. In 1920, he attended the (NCBWA) inaugural meeting in Accra, and returned home to form the Gambia Branch of this

---

[57] See Perfect, D. 'The Political Carrier of E.F Small' in Hughes, A. (Ed). *The Gambia: Studies in Society*, University of Birmingham, 1989, p.60.

pioneer nationalist movement. The NCBWA was a nationalist movement which called for African elected Legislative Council members, equal access to civil service jobs in the colonies, more African influence in the use of tax revenue and the granting of self-rule to the five British West African colonies.

When he returned from Accra, a changed man, Small launched a newspaper dedicated to attacking the repressive colonial policies and colonial excesses such as forced labour and corporal punishment. *The Gambia Outlook and Senegambia Reporter* became the flagship of the Bathurst press and remained undaunted by the numerous attempts to muzzle it by the colonial authorities[58].

His trade union activities were centred on the Bathurst Trade Union which he formed in the 1920s bringing together mainly dock workers. In 1929, Small led them into a successful anti-colonial

---

[58] See Grey-Johnson, N. *Story of the Newspaper*, Banjul, 2004, p.49, 198 for details on the repressive anti press laws of colonial Gambia. See also Grey-Johnson, N. *Small: Watchdog of Society*, Banjul, (2005).

strike which won workers increased minimum wages. The strike rattled the colonial authorities and the European mercantile firms and forced them to agree to periodic review of wages which led to over 100,000 workers in the country securing a twenty-five per cent increase on minimum pay by 1941.

Small won a seat in the Legislative Council in 1947 and was returned in each election till his death in 1958, and mentored many young politicians such as Garba Jahumpa, and George St. Claire Joof who became leading Bathurst politicians in the 1950s onwards.

Small is noted for breaking the Colony – Protectorate divide created by the Colonial authorities to weaken the resolve for unity among the colonised peoples. He took up postings in Ballanghar in 1916, at a time when many Bathurst educated workers would rather resign or get the sack than work up river. His stay in Ballanghar was memorable for he came face to face with the penury and poverty of the provinces caused by neglect of colonial authorities and repression by Chiefs and Commissioners, and this re-awakening must have imbued him with nationalist feelings. In addition, thereafter, he championed the plight of rural peoples by volunteering to write petitions on their behalf when they came into collision with colonial authorities. In this, he became a noted crusader for social justice.

His role in the promotion of social justice and equality became clear in the 1927 Upper Saloum chieftaincy crisis. For three years, he tirelessly supported the cause of a dismissed chief and succeeded in ensuring his reinstatement.

On May 13 1927, Governor Middleton had dismissed Omar Ceesay as Head Chief of Upper Saloum accused of tolerating witch torture in Njau, the district capital, and of attempting to hide it from the Travelling Commissioner North Bank Province, Major Macklin. Governor Middleton also went further to banish the dismissed Chief to

Jamalai, in the Sami District, and seized his medallion awarded two years earlier for good services.

The banished Chief wrote a letter to Small asking for help to be restored to his post as he felt that he was a victim of injustice and colonial high-handedness. Small took up the case and dispatched a ten-page memorandum in defence of the disgraced Saloum Chief to Governor Middleton, and the Secretary of State for Colonies in London. Beside defending the chief against the allegations of the Travelling Commissioner, Small used the petition to reveal the rampant use of forced labour in the district to construct causeways, prisoner deaths due to torture at Georgetown gaol and Major Macklin's ill treatment and hatred for the deposed Chief who had reported Macklin's 'reign of terror' to Governor Armitage. Small's intervention yielded fruit. In October 1929, the deposed Chief was granted audience with Commissioner Middleton and a subsequent inquiry exonerated him. In 1933, Omar Ceesay won the chieftaincy elections and was reinstated. Small had won a big victory against colonial intransigence.

Another blow he landed on colonial arrogance was his successful leadership of the 1929 dockers' strike in Bathurst. For three weeks, the colonial economy was at a standstill as Small led the dock workers on strike over pay and working conditions. Police dogs and teargas could not melt the determination of the workers. The strike ended when the colonial government negotiated a favourable pay rise and longer leave periods for the workers. This strike was the first recorded in the British colonial empire and it put Small firmly on the pedestal of anti-colonial militants.

Mama Tamba Jammeh (1890- 1987): Traditional Leader and Farmer

There are many reasons to justify the assertion that Mama Tamba Jammeh, chief of Illiasa from 1928 to 1966 was one of the greatest rulers of the modern Gambian nation. He embodied tradition, modernity, sagacity and innovation. At a time when only European Colonial officials were capable of owning and driving cars, Mama Tamba owned lorries and cars which plied the roads and causeways he built in his area. When Europeans thought Africans were incapable of increasing the yields of their crops, he boosted rice production in his district making it the first Gambian region to be self-sufficient in food.

He was among the first people in the rural areas of Gambia to attend the Mohammedan school when it was formed in 1903, and he wrote and spoke good English, which never ceased to impress his colonial bosses. He pioneered politics in the protectorate sitting in the legislative council for over a decade, and he was influential in giving women the vote in 1960. He also initiated the annual Mansabengo or chiefs' conferences that were held regularly from 1944 to 1965.

Jammeh was the son of Jatta Selung Jammeh, a Serere-Mandinka, and Awa Jobe, a Wollof.[59] Jatta Selung was one of the top generals of the famous Jihad leader Maba Jahou Bah. When the Baddibu wars ended in the 1870s, Jatta Selung was appointed ruler of the whole of Baddibu by the victorious Maba Jahou, who asked him to form a theocratic state. However, when the British colonialists declared the colonial protectorate in 1894, Jatta Selung was allowed to become the first chief of Illiasa. As a son of a chief, Jammeh attended the Muhammedan School in Bathurst

---

[59] Ceesay, Hassoum. "Jammeh, Mama Tamba." *African American Studies Center*, edited by Ed. . *Oxford AfricaAmerican Studies Center*, http://www.oxfordaasc.com/article/opr/t356/e0049 (accessed Fri Feb 14 14:24:32 EST 2014).

from 1905 to 1913. Soon after, he was employed as a court scribe in his father's tribunal. In 1925, the Travelling Commissioner Ozanne appointed him deputy chief, as his father was infirm and unable to continue with the demanding tasks of his duties. In 1928, his father died and Mama Tamba Jammeh was promoted chief of Illiasa on 28 February 1928.

He remained chief for nearly 40 years and brought much prosperity to himself, his people and his family. Archival records on him and his district compiled by Colonial Commissioner show their acute ambivalence about him. In some instances Jammeh was praised for his intelligence, literacy, foresight and loyalty; yet, in other instances, he was roundly criticized for his strong rule. However, nearer to the end of his long rule, perhaps with the benefit of hindsight, the Governor in Bathurst called him 'one of the best chiefs in the country'. We may add that Jammeh was not an autocrat, if he were, the colonialists would have deposed him. He was above all a strong ruler, who cared so much for his people's welfare that he did as much as possible to create an atmosphere of stability and control. In fact, as we will see later, he was open enough to allow some of his courtiers to openly rebel against him in the 1930s and challenged his rule head on.

Jammeh was a progressive chief. He was concerned with bringing the wherewithal of progress to his people including communication, education, and agriculture. In 1935 he completed the causeway across the famous Bao Bolong creek in his district that was an all season structure which greatly facilitated communication within the district and linked Illiasa with the rest of the country. Before the completion of the causeway, motorists had to wait days for the low tide to risk crossing the water body into Sanjal and Farafenni. As he owned a motorcar himself, the causeway must have greatly helped him to run affairs of his district. Besides this bridge, he also regularly maintained the paths and roads in the area such that colonial officials were able to access his people with more ease than in other parts of the country.

We should also add that such infrastructure greatly helped communication and trade in the area as goods and people were moved much faster.

Jammeh was a devout farmer. He promoted the cultivation of food crops so as to bring about food self-sufficiency. He particularly promoted the cultivation of rice. In 1941, 'he cleared the Kanikunda swamps and established a huge rice project that was described by a visiting colonial official as one of the biggest projects of its kind in British West Africa.'[60] The project was so successful that in 1946 there was 'a 50 per cent increase in rice harvest in the district'.[61] In 1954, Prince Phillips, while visiting the Gambia Colony, visited the rice project to see for himself the success story.[62] Jammeh replicated the project at Bambali and other villages in the region. However, the most visionary decision he ever made concerning boosting

---

[60] Ceesay, H. 'Mama Tamba Jammeh' Oxford African American Studies centre, 2014.

[61] See 'Confidential Report on Chiefs, 1947', Gambia National Archives.

[62] See Ceesay, H. 'Jammeh, Mama Tamba', Oxford African American Studies Center.

agriculture was his fiat in 1943 that all married men in Illiasa must cultivate a rice plot. Hitherto, rice cultivation was seen as a women's role; this decree therefore revolutionized the rice culture in Illiasa and has limitless impact on the production of the grain in the country.

Another important agriculture policy he initiated was the Village Famine Reserve Farms that he started in 1940. In the scheme, he required every village in his domain to cultivate a communal coos farm for consumption during the hungry season that usually lasted from July to September. What must have motivated him to initiate this idea was the fact that famine struck most of rural Gambia during the middle months of the rainy season, which severely impacted the abilities of farmers to grow crops in addition to provide for malnourished women and children. The scheme was, therefore, an emergency food reserve to be tapped only during the lean months of July and August when food reserves in the household were at lowest points. This project, which had the support of the colonial government, greatly improved the nutritional standards of the people of Illiasa. Much earlier in 1939, he had introduced the ox plough to make farming much less strenuous to farmers. The plough enabled farmers to cultivate larger areas in less time and also reduced the drudgery of weeding and harvesting. The success of his experiment led to the colonial government open Ox plough schools in various parts of the country to instruct farmers on the latest farming technologies. The Mixed Farming Centres created by the new PPP Government in the early 1960s to promote rural agriculture also owe a lot to the initial work of Jammeh with the ox ploughs.

In order to better harness the huge livestock resource of his people, in 1941, Jammeh launched a successful cattle immunization programme in his district. In two months, two thousand livestock were inoculated against killer diseases like rinderpest and foot and mouth disease. He used his own vehicle to transport the immunization team to all parts of the district. The following year,

Governor Sir Hillary Blood described the campaign as the most successful ever held in the country.

Jammeh developed the social amenities in his district. He brought a dispensary and market at Balingho and developed Kanikunda as a wharf town and groundnuts depot in 1948. During the Second World War he remained a staunch ally of the British. In the war, he led the Illiasa people to contribute to the war fund with a personal donation of ten pounds. Other village heads and notables in the District also made generous contributions to the War Fund that was used to buy Spitfire bombers to help defend London from Hitler's blitzkrieg. Moreover, he secured one hundred recruits for the Gambia Regiment of the Royal West African Frontier Force, RWAFF, to fight the Allied cause. Throughout the war, Jammeh made regular appeals for his people to remain loyal to Britain and her majesty, especially when Dakar, Senegal, fell into the hands of the Quisling Vichy regime in 1940, which meant that his district was incredibly a few miles away from the Nazi stronghold West Africa.

For his strong support to the Allies, Jammeh was one of dozens of West African traditional rulers, including Nigerian Obas and Sultans, who were invited to attend the victory celebrations organised by the British in London in 1948. The celebrations were used to thank the chiefs for their support in the war against Hitler.

Yet, as mentioned above, his rule was not without hitches. In 1934, Jammeh faced a major challenge in leadership when he survived a palace coup led by his powerful lieutenants Suntung Camara and Tomany Marong who accused him of highhandedness, bribery and other forms of misadministration. The accusations were serious enough to warrant a commission of inquiry, which subsequently led to the exoneration of Jammeh and the jailing of the accusers for perjury. The accusations left a bad sentiment in the district, especially from the villages where the plotters came from.

Jammeh was highly cultured. He spoke many Gambian languages and was fluent in English. He was one of the first Gambians to own a car, a Ford that he bought in 1939 just before the outbreak of the war. His efficiency as a chief encouraged the colonial government to add the village of No Kunda into his district in 1941.

Jammeh was a political figure who played a salient part in Gambian independence politics. From 1947 to 1962, he sat in the Legislative Council as one of the Chief's representatives and he was a founding member of the PPP in 1959. As a legislator he supported rural issues, such as, farming subsidies and the upgrading of Armitage School in 1959. His political influence reached its apogee in February 1958, when he mobilized the chiefs in favour of having Protectorate persons elected into office instead of the Bathurst politicians. His speech at the conference was the end of the dominance of national politics by Bathurst born political leaders. He said:

> We shall take care of ourselves and elect our own candidates from the farmers and chiefs and send them to the Legislative Council... In case of ministers, we expect our Protectorate representatives to be appointed Ministers... We do not desire any help from anyone who is not a member of the Protectorate.[63]

Immediately after these remarks, the Protectorate was divided into twenty voting districts for the 1960 elections, and Bathurst was divided into five electoral areas.

In 1933, a colonial commissioner wrote of Jammeh the following words which could well serve as his epitaph:

> He is a man of character and energy and exercises strict control over the people of his district. His duties are carried out most

[63] See *Gambia Echo*, February, 1958, p.3.

satisfactorily. His roads are cleared first in the provinces and kept in repairs during the rains.[64]

He retired in 1964 and died on 13 October 1987.

[64] See 'Annual Confidence Report on chiefs, 1934', Gambia National Archives.

Wilfred Davidson Carrol (1900-1941): Pioneer Lawyer

When Wilfred Davidson Carrol died on October 30th 1941, at the young age of 41, tributes to him came from all sections of the Bathurst community including Christians, Muslims, Europeans and the Governor Southern. This was a measure of what Carrol meant to the wide gamut of Gambian society by his law practice, political activism and social standing. Indeed, one mourner lamented in the pages of The *Gambia Echo* newspaper, 'our sole remaining joy is gone'.[65] Like his Legislative Council member colleague and fellow lawyer Sir Sam Forster, Carroll was one of the most educated Gambians of his time, and came from a wealthy Bathurst Aku family which had carved a niche for itself in the business circles of the colony for decades before the 1900s. Many of these Aku

---

[65] See Downes-Thomas, Charles Whitfield. 'The Honourable Mr. Wilfred Davidson Carrol: a Memoir', *Gambia Echo*, 10 November 1941.

families wanted to give the best education to their children and worked hard to save to enable their children to go to the world's best institutions of learning. It is credit to these Aku families that Gambia produced a highly capable and talented small pool of professionals in the early 1900s, when few Africans had a chance of seeing the inside of a classroom.

Carrol's father, Henry Richmond Carrol, established a provisions and hardware shop in Bathurst in 1883, and traded upriver in groundnuts and timber until his death in 1913. His mother Anne Maria Forster was daughter to, another Aku notable, Samuel Forster. Following primary education in Bathurst and Freetown, Carrol entered Oxford University in 1920 and graduated with a law degree in 1924; he was called to the English Bar as a Barrister in 1925. In 1924, he was elected the first President of the newly formed West African Students Union (WASU), the student body of English speaking students in the UK and America. He led WASU in great stride and put the nascent association, which was the mill that churned up the cream of West African leaders, including Nkrumah and Azikwe, on a sound footing. His exposure to students' politics inspired him to return home to set up practice and take up the challenge of leadership which Gambia was so desperately needed at this time.

Back home, his law firm 'Carrol and Company', was the most successful indigenous legal enterprise which represented a wide range of Gambians irrespective of religion or origins.[66] He won the hearts of the Protectorate people by offering free legal services to distressed people at loggerheads with the colonial authorities. He was the first lawyer to travel upriver to defend clients before the Provincial courts presided by Travelling Commissioners. He single-handedly drafted the Gambia Criminal Code in 1931, and with Sir Samuel Forster, campaigned for its acceptance by the local people who had reservations about its

[66] See Ceesay, H. "Carrol, Wilfred Davidson." *African American Studies Center*, edited by Ed. . *Oxford African American Studies Center*

application. It is important that we point out that the majority of the Bathurst elite loathed the new Criminal Code and they feared that it would introduce 'new offences and new penalties and would sweep away existing legal safeguards'.[67] Therefore, it was fiercely opposed, especially by E.F Small's Rate Payers Association, as another case of legal tyranny on the people. In his newspaper, Small lamented the fact that while Nigerian, Sierra Leonean African legislative members vehemently opposed codification, Carrol and Forster remained silent on the issue when it was tabled by Governor Richards in 1932 and did not lift a finger against the enactment of the Code in 1934. Carrol was a consummate lawyer, whose court appearances were a sight to behold; his rich Oxford accent and analytical power encouraged his colleagues to respect and admire him.

To his credit, he combined a rewarding legal career with a vigorous political life which started in 1931 when he won the Jollof Town South seat in the

[67] Downes-Thomas, 1941

BUDC. In 1933, Carrol sought re-election but was roundly defeated by Small's RPA candidates amidst accusation that Carrol bribed voters. In 1934, he was appointed into the Legislative Council where he met Sir Samuel Forster and Sheikh Omar Faye. Carrol proved his mettle as a staunch defender of the rights of his people and a lucid debater. He threw himself wholeheartedly into the affairs of the Council and soon became the proponent of better working conditions for civil servants and the rural masses. In an address to the Council in 1937, he lamented the poor price that the mercantile firms were paying for produces like ground nuts and bee wax and also opposed the introduction of Income Tax in 1940 to raise money for the British war effort. Instead, he asked the government to pay allowances to children of civil servants as was the case in Nigeria and Ghana to reduce the burden of dependence on government workers. In 1940, he charged the colonial government of neglect of the prisoners and suggested increase in ration and introduction of library facilities for inmates.

Carrol's other public activities included Deputy Coroner, Crown Prosecutor, Member of the Board of Education, and service on the Committee to Advice on Prisoners Detained Under the War Time Emergency; this made him the Gambia's first human rights lawyer. As Deputy Coroner, one of his last duties involved an inquest into an abandoned baby at Half Die and the reporting of which put John Findain Dailey, the crusading editor of *Weekly News* into trouble with the authorities.

Carrol was a socialite who belonged to many clubs such as the Bathurst Optimist Club, Reform Club and the Tip-Toe Club.[68] Many a Bathurst soiree owed its success to Carrol's Master of Ceremonies prowess. He was a staunch Methodist and was a member of the District Synod. He was widely travelled; like all cultured Aku men of his time, he could not miss a holiday visiting friends and

---

[68] See 'Carrol, Davidson Wilfred', *Oxford African American Studies Center.*

relatives along the Coast and in the UK. In 1930, he married Margot Blain and they had one daughter.

Although of poor health since the death of his wife in 1937, his sudden death in 1941[69] sent shock waves in the Bathurst community. Carrol's death came so close to that of another notable African, Sir Samuel Forster and it was a moment of combined loss of African leadership in the Gambia. This could have had a negative impact on the aspirations for political, social and economic advancement. A large section of the community felt that The Gambia was now bereft of a strong voice of reason in the Legislature and in the corridors of colonial power. However, the deaths also afforded an opportunity for the colonial government to widen political rights, an example being the franchise to Gambians. Hitherto, Legislative Council members were nominated by the Governor. The question was, for certain Bathurst elitists; would the replacements of Forster and Carrol be found through elections? Sadly, no;

[69] See, Hughes and Perfect, *Historical Dictionary*, p.31-32

as it took another six years before the first elections were held to elect members to the legislature. However, with his death came a political soul searching that started off the inexorable move of the Colony towards the franchise and eventual independence in 1965. Moreover, the demise of Carrol and his uncle, Sir Samuel Forster, paved the way for the eventual rise of E.F Small into mainstream politics after three decades of agitation.

Upon Carrol's death, his colleagues, African and European, paid tribute to him in the Bathurst Daily:

> A great power of leadership and a career of service has been lost. He was a man of dynamic personality, unusual ability, breadth of vision and unflagging zeal.[70]

---

[70] Downes, Thomas, 1941.

Imam Momodou Lamin Bah (1906-1983): Religious Scholar

The date of birth of Imam Momodou Lamin Bah is not very clear. According to the Dictionary of African Biographies (1970) Imam Bah was born on 12th March 1910, while an obituary in the *Senegambia Sun* of December, 1983, states 1906 as his year of birth. But it is unarguable that he was born in Bathurst, the descendant of a highly respected Muslim family that traced its links to the great jihadist Saer Matty Bah, the scion of Maba Jahu Bah, who brought Islam to the Soninkes of the North Bank and the Jolas of Foni.

At the age of seven, Imam Bah was sent to read the Islamic scriptures in the sub region. In Kaolack, he studied at the respected Niassene seminary under the tutorship of Khalifa Abdoulie Niasse. While in Tivavoune, he read Arabic language, literature, history and arts under the professorship of the venerable Sheikh Alhajie Malick Sy, the exponent of the Tijaniyya brotherhood in Senegambia. Imam Bah also read Islamic jurisprudence, and attained the Higher Diploma in Islamic Pedagogy in 1938. A further measure of his academic profundity was his specialisation in the study of the Biography of Prophet Muhammad.

Upon his return from studies, he was employed as an Islamic teacher at the Department of Education. For twenty five years he taught in numerous schools in and around Bathurst. In this capacity, Imam Bah followed the footsteps of his grandfathers, being an indefatigable propagator of Islam and knowledge of the Holy Q'uran.

In 1949, Imam Bah was appointed Deputy Imam of Bathurst Central Mosque. In 1958, he ascended to the venerable role of Chief Imam and chairman of the Gambia Imam Board. The hallmarks of his tenure were the regular annual renditions and translations of the Holy Q'uran on behalf of the Gambia Muslim Association. He was able to maintain the unity of the Bathurst Muslim community and fostered religious tolerance and impartiality. Such ideals were highly precious in the heated Bathurst pre-Independence politics when ethnicity and religion were trump cards for the new politicians.

In recognition of his untiring efforts to promote Islam in The Gambia and the sub region, Imam Bah received several merits and medals. In 1960, he was awarded the *Order Nationale du Senegal* by Momodou Dia, the Senegalese prime minister. In 1971, he was given the Order of the Republic of The Gambia by President Jawara. Imam Bah officiated prayers during momentous occasions in Gambian history including the 1965 Independence celebrations and the marriage of Sir Dawda Jawara to Lady Chilel in 1967. He also served as patron of the Gambia Muslim Association.

Imam Bah was a member of the Executive Council of the World Muslim League based in Saudi Arabia. As head of the Hajj Committee, he pioneered the use of airplanes by Gambian pilgrims. He showed great leadership skills in 1969, when amidst the controversy surrounding the miniskirt; he decided to convene an unprecedented congregation of one hundred and twenty five imams from all over the country to advise Government on the issues. The Imams condemned the miniskirt as 'immoral and unethical'[71]. However, the controversy had deep political undertones as it was frequently suggested in the press that the PPP government was resisting pressure to ban the miniskirt because it did not want to alienate urban women voters in the April 1970 Republican Referendum. However, the Imam's intervention helped to cool off the heated controversy.

---

[71] See ' Imams condemned immoral dancing', *The Gambia News Bulletin* 30 September 1969, p. 1, reports the historic Imams meeting held at the Crab Island School, Banjul. The Imams also condemned the *mbabas* dancing with the miniskirt. See also, Ceesay, Hassoum. '*Gambian Women: An Introductory History*, p.103.

Imam Bah passed away on 3 December 1983. In a eulogy, the Gambia Muslim Association wrote:

> He will long be remembered for his erudition, his steadfastness for truth and understanding among Gambian Muslims.[72]

[72] See *Senegambia Sun*, (Banjul), February 1983, p.1

Father Thomas Gregory Jobe (1906-1995): Church Leader

Father Thomas Gregory Jobe was one of the pioneer Gambian Catholic priests in the 1920-1930s who helped to plant the seeds of Christianity in The Gambia. Born in Bathurst 1906 of Wollof father and Mullato mother, Thomas Jobe attended the Methodist Boys High School which he left in 1922 at the top of his class. At this early age, Jobe dedicated his life to the work of the Church and was sent to the famous Ngasobil Seminary in Senegal where he met and befriended Leopold Sedar Senghor, future Poet-President of Senegal.[73] After further seminary studies in France, Jobe was ordained a Priest in Paris in 1933. He returned home in 1934 to serve his people.

---

[73] See Frederiks, M. *We Have Toiled all Night: history of Christianity in The Gambia*, Boekencentrum, 2001.

Father William Cleary wrote in his book *Reaping A Rich Harvest* (1990) that the first Christians to reach the Gambia were the Portuguese who first arrived in 1456. They settled first at James Island and its mainland towns such as Juffureh, Albreda and Sika where they practiced peacefully along with their Muslim neighbours. The Portuguese built the earliest churches at Geregia, San Domingo and Albreda, remains of which still stand today. As the Portuguese trading population spread to other upriver towns such as Bintang, their Christian influence also went with them and by the mid-16th century, there was a large Christian population of Portuguese traders, Mullatos and a few local converts. Conversion was not definitely the priority of the early Europeans; they were pre-occupied with enlarging their trading sphere, and locked in internecine wars for control of strategic trade locations such as James Island. Thus, Christianity did not take root in the upriver settlements. Moreover, as the European trader population was itinerant, their religious influence was not pronounced.

It was only after 1816, when Bathurst was made a permanent settlement by the British that the first resident Christian populations arrived: Catholics from Senegal (mainly Wollof artisans); Anglicans from the British officials, soldiers, and Methodists from the Liberated African Populations (Aku).However, the early Christian populations suffered from the dearth of priests such that in many occasions personnel had to be borrowed from Senegal to preside over mass in Bathurst. The high mortality rate among European priests and the slow penetration of the faith into the predominantly Muslim population were setbacks that the early Christian populations had to endure. In the early 1900s, as the local adherents increased, it was deemed necessary by all the churches to train a solid core of local priests who would work side by side with their European colleagues. There was an attempt to Gambianise the church clergy. Among the first local priests to be ordained was Father Charles Mendy in 1922; followed by Father Edwin Paul and Father Gregory Thomas Jobe in

1933. Sadly, mortality, again, devastated this new generation of Gambian priests as Mendy died in 1935, and Edwin in 1932. Father Jobe was left to carry the torch of local priesthood.

Jobe's first mass in Bathurst was conducted in Wollof and attracted much praise from his flock who were not unaccustomed to having mass in their own languages. For the next ten years, he worked with Father Meehan to spread Catholicism in Bathurst and upriver and the Kombos. Father Jobe did notable work among the Serere in Mbollet, where he did not only win converts but also with Meehan established the first experimental farms and aviaries in the country. In 1937, they opened the school in the village. He, together with father Whiteside, were pioneer priests at Bwiam in 1935 and by dint of hard work, made it into one of the most active missions in the country.

In 1944, he had a dispute with Father Meehan over alleged racism and Jobe left for Senegal where he continued to preach in Casamance until 1946. It is believed that Father Jobe had become very popular among the local congregations and, therefore, he increasingly wanted more freedom and not to be dictated by the White boss. This naturally brought differences between him and Father Meehan.

In 1947, Father Jobe left for France and did not return to Africa until 1960 when Senghor invited him to join the diplomatic service of independent Senegal. He served as Ambassador in Rome and Ghana, Ivory Coast until his retirement. In 1975, he returned to The Gambia to live a quiet life, mainly helping to train catechists. Father Jobe died in 1995.

Momodou Musa Njie (1908-1993): Business Magnate

The adage, from rags to riches, has never been truer for any Gambians than for Alhagie Momodou Musa N'jie, the Gambia's first millionaire. Momodou Musa, as he was popularly known, rose from cattle herding to petty trading and ended up as one of Black Africa's most successful business magnates. He dabbled in import-export trade, real estate and gems dealing. His career was as interesting as it was phenomenal: a successful entrepreneur, political heavy weight and a family man with 40 children.

Momodou Musa was born in Basse, URD circa 1908, of cattle-rearing Fula origin. He spent his early years herding his father's large cattle stock in the low lands of Basse Santu Su. At the tender age of 18, Musa became an apprentice to Ibrahim Salman, a Lebanese business tycoon in Basse. Musa soon proved his entrepreneurial skills by expanding Salman's business from wholesale and retail to dealing in livestock, cola nuts, gunpowder and diamonds[74]. In the mid-1940s, he separated from Salman to start his own business. And thence, his way was paved in gold.

He trekked around the sub region buying and selling assorted goods. He bought cattle from Mali, cola nuts from lower Guinea, gun powder from Casamance. Later, he ventured further into Ghana where he traded in gold and into Nigeria from where he brought timber into The Gambia. Momodou Musa had become the colony's first international businessman.

By mid-1948 when he had gathered enough expertise to run his growing enterprises, Musa moved to Bathurst. His early years were tough: the Lebanese, Syrian and European trading companies dominated both the retail and the wholesale

---

[74] See 'The Grand Old man of Banjul Dies', *Gambia Weekly*, 6 July 1990, p.3.

business sector and they had the support of the colonialists and the local bank of British West Africa. But with determination and crystal sharp intelligence, Musa soon seized control of the import market for consumables like rice, flour, sugar. He pioneered the importation of cement into The Gambia in 1950

In 1951, he extended his business tentacles to East Africa and the Far East and traded in coffee in Kenya, raw tobacco in Malawi and electronic goods in Singapore and Hong Kong, all of them British colonies. His monumental business success aroused the suspicion of the British colonialists who could not believe that an unlettered colonial subject like Momodou Musa, from a very modest origin in the protectorate, could become so successful in business.

In addition, Musa's success dealt a blow to the colonialists' prejudice that Africans were not yet ready to manage their political and economic affairs. Here was a man whose little knowledge of

English was at best unintelligible, but who controlled so many enterprises with managerial skills that even a Harvard Business School graduate would envy.

No historian, except perhaps Berkeley Rice, author of *Enter The Gambia* Fame, has yet mentioned Musa's contribution to the anti-colonial struggle in The Gambia. The man was a nationalist, in his own peculiar way.

He fought colonialism by encouraging dozens of other Gambians, particularly those from the protectorates, into business who later gave support to young nationalist politicians in their electoral campaigns. First Republic politicians like M.C Cham passed through his tutelage and he acted as Godfather to them which made them retain their parliamentary seats for decades.[75]

---

[75] See 'The Grand Old Man of Banjul Dies', *Gambia Weekly*, 6 July 1990.

Another contribution of Musa to The Gambia's struggle for independence was his steely support to nationalist politicians like P.S Njie, the leader of the United Party and Chief Minister from 1961-62. Musa bankrolled the UP on several crucial occasions, including the allimportant 1962 elections. It was largely due to his influence that the UP dominated the URD from 1960- 1966. His support also nourished prominent UP politician like the firebrand MC Cham, who rose to become deputy party leader in 1970. Such conspicuous nationalist leanings made the British colonialists to clamp down on Musa's business on several occasions.

On one September morning in 1952, the Colonial Secretary, acting under orders from Governor Percy Wyn Harris, ordered Bathurst police to raid the house of Musa to look for a money printing contraption which the British suspected him of owning. They assiduously frisked Musa's rooms but could not see any currency forging machine. Undaunted, Musa, approached Lawyer P.S Njie who sued the British officials on his behalf. Thereafter P.S Njie, the well-dressed Bathurst politician became a close associate of Musa the wealthy businessman. This association translated into tacit support for Njie's political adventures, until Musa abandoned U.P in 1966 complaining of P.S Njie's showmanship.

The Njie-Musa breakup was to sound the funeral bugles of the UP; when he left the UP, several other MPs like M.C Jallow and M.C Cham left the party for the PPP.

In 1967, Musa 'agreed to join the ruling PPP and to consummate his support; he gave his daughter, the elegant Chilel Njie of age 17, to Prime Minister, DK Jawara, for his wife'.[76] The Prime Minister was then the country's most eligible bachelor having just won a divorce suit against his first consort, Lady Hannah Augusta Mahoney (died 1981) in a London court. Prime Minister Jawara's marriage to Chilel

---

[76] See Ceesay, H. 'Momodou Musa Njie' Oxford African American Studies Centre', 2014.

soon began to pay political dividends. His wealthy father-in-law spared no effort to canvass support for the PPP, albeit in his peculiar discreet style. By 1968, the first couple had their first child, and with it a fabulous political trophy in the person of I.M Garba Jahumpa, the Bathurst leftist politician, friend of Musa who merged his Muslim Congress Party with the PPP. Musa's entry into the PPP was indeed a boost for the party.

Strangely, Musa seldom used his direct connections to State House to curry favours for friends or family. Instead, he used his fabulous wealth for philanthropy. He built mosques in various places in the country, including on Picton Street, Banjul; sent people to hajj and sponsored 'daaras' and 'dairas'.[77] Berkeley Rice wrote that in 1965, Musa spent £4,200 to sponsor people to do the hajj. He also built charitable homes for his Fula ilk to stay in when they were in Banjul. But perhaps his greatest single philanthropic act was £2,800 (D240.000 in today's money) independence

[77] Muslim religious prayer associations

gift to The Gambia on February 19, 1965. Musa personally handed over the cheque for the amount to the Gambian Prime Minister saying rather humbly, 'This is my small gift to The Gambia on this good day.'[78]

Musa successfully nurtured 20 sons and 20 daughters. He had them by four wives. He educated most of them in the most respected universities in the world: Oxford, Cambridge and Harvard.[79] As the initiator of the lucrative re-export trade which has since become the mainstay of The Gambian economy, Musa has craved for himself a lofty spot in the economic history of The Gambia. For his monumental role in developing entrepreneurship, he was decorated with Order of the Republic of The Gambia in 1975 and in 1987. President Abdou Diouf of Senegal also decorated him with an insignia. Musa died on the 4th July 1993 at a London clinic at the age of 82. In 1964, he told a visiting New York Times journalist: "I go

---

[78] Rice, B. *Enter The Gambia*, 1967.

[79] See, Ceesay, H. 'Momodou Musa Njie'. Edited by African-American Studies Centre, 2014

buy good here. I go sell them there. I go buy there. I sell them here. I bring more, sell more. That's my life[80]."

[80] See Rice, B. *Enter The Gambia: birth of an improbable Nation*, Houghton Mifflin, 1967, p.261. See also, Grey-Johnson, N. 'Death of a Baron' *Topic Magazine*(Banjul) July 1990, p.5-9 for a critique of Musa's business tactics and philanthropic work.

P.S. Njie (1909-1993): Nationalist Politician

Pierre Sam Nije was the dominant figure in Gambian politics from 1951 to 1962. His United Party (UP) led the struggle for independence from its formation in 1951 to its defeat in the 1962 elections. He has been described by some historians as the best leader The Gambia never had. He was a lawyer, an intellectual and most notably, a nationalist politician.

Njie was born in 1909 in Bathurst of Muslim Wolof parents. He was educated at the Catholic Mission school of St. Augustine. In 1939 he converted to Catholicism. He worked as a civil servant and in 1943 he joined the army. Between 1944 and 1948 he studied law in London and upon his return he opened a flourishing law firm.

He entered politics in 1951, when he contested the Legislative Council election for Bathurst and lost.

He then decided to build his power base by forming the United Party which soon became the strongest party in the colony and had a substantial following in the protectorate. At the inception of the party, he told followers that the UP was a 'party for all Gambians and all friends of The Gambia who are interested in the development of the country. This is not a party for any race, tribe or religion.'[81]

His 1954 manifesto was based on improving the economic status of Gambians by giving farmers better producer prices for their crops and increased salaries for Civil Servants[82]. Njie won one of the Legislative seats for Bathurst and was made Minister of Education in the first Gambian Cabinet. However, he was dismissed in December 1955 for making allegations against the Gambia Police Force which he accused of maltreating his party supporters. As he was unable to prove his

---

[81] See *Gambia Echo* 5 July 1954, p.1.

[82] For the details of this interesting Manifesto, see G*ambia Echo* 13 September 1954, p. 1-2. See also Ceesay, H. 'P.S Njie' in Senghor, J (ed). *Gambia's Five Giants*, Africa World Press (forthcoming).

allegations before a subsequent enquiry, he was also temporally suspended from the bar and disrobed.

Soon afterwards Njie went into self-exile in the UK where he remained until 1959. He led his party in the 1960 general elections in which his party won all the seats in the colony and four out of twelve seats in the Protectorate. He was offered a post in the Cabinet which he rejected. However, when the Government collapsed in 1961, he was appointed the Chief Minister and allowed to appoint a Cabinet. His tenure although short was quite fruitful.

He played a crucial role in the shaping of the 1962 Constitution. He led his party's delegation to the all-important Constitutional Talks in 1961. His government also built the Leprosy Centre at Mile 2, the power station at Basse and the Brumen Bridge in 1962 at the cost of £85,600. More importantly, he prioritized the radio service for the Gambia leading to the establishment of Radio Gambia in May 1962.

The Brikama-Mansakonko road was also upgraded and his government's response to the devastating floods in Basse in 1961 was also highly praised. During his tenure, Njie also worked towards closer co-operation between Banjul and Senegal which culminated in the Senegalo-Gambienne meeting in 1963. Soon after his appointment as Chief Minister in March 1961, Njie attended the Senegalese Independence celebrations where he held talks with Prime Minister Dia on bilateral co-operations. In June 1961, he led the delegation to the first Gambia – Senegal inter-ministerial meeting held in Dakar. This body was meant to formulate and harmonized policies meant for closer co-operation between the two states.

As Chief Minister, he welcomed Queen Elizabeth II to The Gambia in 1961, and was credited with the successful tour. When he lost power in 1962, P.S. Njie's political fortunes began to dim and within a year over half of his MPs had defected to the PP. Indeed by 1956 the UP had only six members in the House. The 1965 referendum on a republican constitution gave him a chance to recoup his political lustre. He effectively campaigned against the constitution leading to its rejection in November 1965. He believed that an executive president would introduce single party dictatorship in the country, and he thought that The Gambia was too economically dependent on Britain to go alone.

However, his success in the referendum failed to materialize into a UP victory in the 1966 general elections which the party lost with a reduced vote. Following this defeat, Njie's leadership of the party came under attack leading to yet more defections. By 1970 the party had split with his brother E.D. Njie leading the breakaway faction which blamed P.S. for the party's misfortune. The party's campaign against the 1970 republican constitution failed.

Njie contested the 1972 elections only as a parliamentary candidate and not as the UP Presidential candidate. Although he won his seat he lost it few months later on grounds of absenteeism. This brought an end to Njie's illustrious political career. He led a flamboyant political life and had the common touch with ordinary people; however his refusal to broker closer ties with the PPP alienated him from his own supporters. He spent the late years of his life in seclusion surrounded by his extensive large library.

While in power, Njie was widely trusted as an honest, trustworthy personality by colleagues including colonial officials. He was always well dressed and well read. His favourite book was The *Gulag Archipelago* by the Russian writer Aleksandra Solzhenitsyn and he also enjoyed poetry by Lord Byron and Shakespeare. In a press interview published in 1990, he explained why he allowed himself to be removed from parliament in these words:

> I can satisfy the electorates without going to the parliament; delegations of my constituencies came to me then and advise

> me to get out of the ridiculousness that was parliament and the political scene at the time. Violations of procedure...[83]

Njie was the first mainstream Gambian politician to break the colony protectorate divide as far as his political base was concern. The UP had strong political support in all parts of the Gambia as evident in the 1960 elections when it won four seats in the colony and four seats in the protectorate unlike the other political parties like the PPP whose political support derived mainly from the protectorate or the Congress Party of Garba Jahumpa which was basically a Bathurst Party.

An editorial in *The Gambia Outlook* of March 27, 1961 said of him, 'he alone is capable of the enormous task bestowed on him'. Upon his death in December 1993, Senegal president Abdou Diouf eulogized him thus:

[83] See *Topic Magazine*, Gambia, August 1990 p.5-19. This was a wide ranging interview Njie gave to Nana Grey-Johnson, The first such interview Njie gave in two decades.

He nurtured the Gambian political scene with his vast knowledge and experience. He was a politician who always worked for the development of his country.[84]

[84] See 'P.S Njie Dies' in *Daily Observer*, Banjul, December 15 1993.

S.H.O Jones (1910-1990) First Gambian Director of Health Services

Dr. Samuel H.O. Jones was a man of many 'firsts'. He was the first Gambian to benefit from Government scholarship in 1927, the first Gambian Director of Medical Services and the first Gambian Chairman of the Public Service Commission (PSC) after independence. His role in the evolution of the country therefore transcended the major sectors of health, administration and politics. He was for several decades before independence one of a handful of Gambians who occupied senior Government positions and was influential in national life. His early life and education were as remarkable as his career in adult life.

Jones was born in 1910 to Maryann Gabbidon and Horton Jones, both of them wealthy Aku merchants in Bathurst at the turn of the last century. He attended the Dobson Street School, and followed in the steps of the children of rich Akus by going to Freetown to complete his secondary schooling. He completed his Cambridge Senior Examinations at the prestigious CMS Grammar School and during his graduation the guest speaker, Governor Middleton of The Gambia spotted him and was so impressed by his performance that he offered young Jones half scholarship to study medicine in the UK. With support from his mother, he completed his course in Medicine and Surgery to return home in 1936 amidst much jubilation in Bathurst[85]. In appreciation of his successful studies, a series of welcoming parties were held by Aku families in his honour. Reporting on the party of the Oldfields *The Gambia Echo* wrote:

> Dr Jones has a retiring modesty.. He is not spoilt by success nor denationalized by his contact with the White race. He is indeed a laudable tribute[86].

---

[85] See 'Our Young Medical Officer' *Gambia Echo*, 20 April 1936, p.1

[86] See *Gambia Echo*, May 11, 1936.

Jones was only the second Gambian trained medical doctor at the time. He spent many years at the new Bansang hospital as medical officer, and upon the death of Dr Richards in 1946, was transferred to Bwiam as medical officer for Kombo and Foni. His tenure as a Medical Officer at the Victoria Hospital in Bathurst from 1948 to 1955 was worthwhile. Under his watch the hospital which was opened in 1854, was renovated and enlarged to one hundred and· eighty beds, with three doctors, one dentist, eighty five dispensers and sixty midwives in 1954.

It is important to discuss the perilous medical condition of the country during this time so as to be able to properly contextualise the Herculean task that medical doctors like Dr Jones had to confront. In the colonial period, medical services were almost non-existent for the majority of Gambians. This led to high infant and maternal mortality rates. For much of the 1940s for example, with a 10 percent patient death rate, more

Gambians living in Bathurst were dying than were born. In 1941, out of one thousand seven hundred and thirty in-patients at the Bathurst Royal Victoria Hospital, one hundred and seventy died. In 1942, one hundred and eighty five out of one thousand eight hundred and fifteen in-patients died at the same hospital. In 1942, there were four hundred and ninety live births registered in Bathurst, and five hundred and ninety one deaths recorded. In 1943, five hundred and thirty nine live births were recorded in the Bathurst Hospital, compared to five hundred and thirty three deaths in the same hospital.

A look at the Bathurst newspapers at the time will also reveal that life was short and painful for most Gambians, especially children and women. For example, between September 23rd 1930 and November 25th 1930, a total of sixty three burial permits were issued for the Bathurst cemetery. (In the colonial days, Gambians had to be issued burial permits before they could bury their dead.

The statistics remained grim throughout the 1930s, 40s and 50s. Most of the deaths were women and children. This high death rate was largely due to the preventable diseases like malaria and yellow fever and also due to malnutrition. The Protectorate was ravaged by outbreaks of Small pox, yellow fever and measles. The handful of medical officers had a daunting task.

By dint of dedication to duty, Dr. Jones rose through the ranks to become Director of Medical Services in 1952[87].An observer celebrated his promotion and described him as 'one of the most successful medical practitioners in the Gambia, and a keen administrator'. This was the start of the process of an indigenous civil service when the colonial authorities were already eager to give independence to their colonies and were keen to replace Europeans with qualified Gambians as head of key Government departments. Indeed, by

[87] See Sagnia, B.K. 'The Development of Parliamentary Democracy in The Gambia' , *Gambia Weekly*, 26 January 1990, p.8, it is stated that he sat in the Executive Council from 1952 onwards.

1952 observers noted that changes in African representation in government were moving more rapidly in the Gambia than in other colonies in West Africa. Customs, Post Office, Treasury and Veterinary departments were all headed by Africans. Dawda Jawara, who became Director of Veterinary Services in 1956, was another beneficiary of this policy. The labour shortages occasioned by the World War Two in the UK, made it prudent that Britain kept its qualified personnel at home to help with post war reconstruction rather than deploy them in the colonies. This was the rationale for the policy of Africanisation. However, the major government Committees and Boards were still largely European in composition.

As Director, Dr. Jones made notable contributions to the development of the medical sector particularly in the areas of research on malaria, TB and leprosy. Also, he decentralized medical facilities such that at his retirement in 1964, there were ten health centres and thirty dispensaries in provincial towns.

From 1952-1962, Jones sat in the Legislative Council, and from 1952-1960 he sat in the Executive Council as a senior Gambian Civil Servant. It was due to his experience in politics that he was asked to organize the landmark 1960 elections, the first under universal adult suffrage. All the political parties, including the failures, acclaimed the results. His third foray into politics came in 1972, when he was nominated speaker of the House of Representatives. He presided over the legislature with vigour and impartiality, even though this was a low point in Gambian opposition politics when the near demise of the United Party had created the situation of a de facto single party system. Dr. Jones executed the unique step of expelling opposition leader P.S Njie from the House for absenteeism ending a brilliant but unfulfilled political career. However, just midway into the life of the 1972-1977 legislature, the slumberous political terrain was given rejuvenation by the new opposition National Convention Party (NCP) led by erstwhile PPP senior minister Sheriff Dibba.

Jones retired from public life in 1977 and passed away in 1990.

Abdou Saidykhan (1910-1968): The Great Hippo Hunter

The art of hunting hardly makes a national hero even though it is one of the world's oldest occupations and providers of sustenance. Hunting is also a means of ensuring security for humans against beasts; it is in this regard that Abdou Saidykhan excelled to earn his place in The Gambia's folklore and history[88].

Saidykhan specialized in hunting hippopotami, the largest mammal on land. Lore has it that during his hippo hunting career, which lasted some thirty years, Abdou Saidykhan killed over two hundred hippos in creeks and swamps of the River Gambia. Armed with a single barrel gun and pouches of gunpowder and trigger caps, he roamed the North Bank of the River Gambia to respond to the calls of

---

[88] See 'Abdou Saidykhan', *Daily Observer* 13-15 November 1998, p.11.

distressed rice fielders, mainly women, whose crop was being devoured by hippos. He did not charge a cent for his dangerous undertakings. Indeed, here lay his philanthropy, in addition to the fact that he shared among riverine people the meat of the hippos he killed. Considering that there was a period of famine in the protectorate due partly to World War Two food rationing and requisition, Abdou's generosity was a livelihood to many people. But who was this great hunter, and as you will see later, soldier, Abdou Saidykhan?

Abdou was born in the village of Faraba, in Fulladu West District, Maccarthy Island Division, in June 1925. Aged 18, he enlisted in the Second Battalion of the Gambia Regiment and fought the Japanese in the sweaty jungles of Burma and the Philippines during the Second World War. Because of his unalloyed gallantry and spotless marksmanship, he rose through the Regiment ranks to become a sergeant. After the end of the war, he demobilized, returned to take up hunting hippos, wreaking untold havoc on rice fields along the North Bank of the river. In fact, the hippo menace was so severe that certain settlements in Sami and Niami districts were put to flight to neighbouring Senegal as wildlife refugees.

Therefore, Abdou's bravery and dedication to cull these pests was highly applauded by the affected people who shared their gratitude in songs and praises in his honour. Also, his exploits soon became legendary. It is believed for example, that he only used a single shot to subdue even the most ferocious hippo and "after shooting he would dive into the water and on surfacing would bring the hippo's tail with him[89]".

He kept the hippos' tails and would occasionally parade them before villagers, district chiefs and commissioners as proof of his daring exploits. The weight of such proof encouraged the colonial commissioners to grant Abdou a yearly ration of gunpowder for his work. And he always lived up

---

[89] See *Gambia News Bulletin*, 9 March, 1968, for a full report on his final days and funeral rites.

to expectations for he respected and loved his occupation. Another legend tells how Abdou would spend several days and nights in the swamps or huddled inside a dugout in order to waylay a hippo. A legend has it that the great hunter reserved much regard for the protection of nature since he avoided shooting hippo cubs, pregnant or aged hippo, or crocodiles.

But perhaps the most interesting legend about the famous hunter concerns his death on Monday 7th March 1968. It states:

> Abdou and his friend left the village of Jarume Koto, Sami district, where they were living on Monday to hunt at Sully Balong. On seeing a hippo, Abdou aimed but before he could fire, another hippo appeared from behind and overturned the canoe. Both occupants fell into the water. The friend swam to the river bank, but the valiant hunter Abdou was nowhere to be seen. Repeated calls, whistles, codes, shouts

> and searches for him were made but to no avail. As night fell, the friend climbed up a tree and remained there until he was found by passing fishermen who took him to Kuntaur. There he told his nightmarish story to the chief and a search was mounted. After four days of frantic searching, Abdou's body was eventually found by the river bank at Kuntaur, in the presence of the commissioner, the chief of Kuntaur and a large crowd.[90]

The news of Abdou Saidykhan's death was greeted with disbelief and sadness. Disbelief because it was impossible to imagine that Abdou Khan, the great hippo hunter, who dared the huge animals so much that he wrestled with them in their domain underwater to slash off their tails as prize, would be killed by the riverside. Planters had looked up to him to save them from the voracious beasts which trampled their livelihood into pieces.

---

[90] *Gambia News Bulletin*, 12 March 1968, p.1

In recognition of such efforts, several Gambians paid tribute to and mourned Abdou Saidykhan. One senior government official said:

> Abdou was great man and a national figure known for his courage and skill in hippo hunting. His death is great loss to rice growers in the McCarthy Island Division whose fields he had protected from hippos for many years.[91]

Recognition of his courage came in 1982 when his life story became a subject of study in Gambian primary schools.

[91] *Gambia News Bulletin*, 12 March 1968.

Chief Omar Mbacke (1912-1994): Nationalist Politician and Traditional Ruler

In a eulogy published soon after the death of Chief Omar Mbacke, Jay Saidy described him as the "most influential and charismatic political figure of the pre-independence era"[92]. This indeed was a fitting accolade to the chief who, for a decade, exploited his political shrewdness to stamp the influence of chiefs on the canvass of pre-independent Gambian politics. He negotiated for an increase in the political representation of chiefs during the constitutional reviews of 1954, 1959 and 1962 and represented the traditional rulers in cabinet for four years in the early 1960s. Indeed, his life was that of a pioneer educationist, a reform

[92] See *The Point*, September 1994 for a tribute by the great Gambian writer Jay Saidy; see also, 'Chief Omar Mbacke', Hassoum Ceesay, *Weekend Observer*, 31 January 1997.

minded traditional chief and moreover, a nationalist politician.

Chief Omar Mbacke began his political career in 1951 as one of the three representatives of the chiefs in the Legislative Council. Their representation in the legislature had been provided for in The Gambia Constitution (Amendment) Order, 1951, following a strong lobby by chiefs during their fifth conference in 1950. The increased representation of chiefs in the legislature was also facilitated by their numerous deputations to the Secretary of State for Colonies. These deputations were largely instigated by Chief Omar Mbacke. He sat in the legislative council for three years during which time he articulated the concerns of the protectorate people and the traditional establishment who were an important appendage in British colonial rule.

Further constitutional amendment in 1954 provided for an Executive Council with Gambian Members to be chaired by the colonial Governor.

Chief Omar Mbacke was nominated to the Council as Minister-without-Portfolio. In the Executive Council, he continued to be the main spokesman for the protectorate people in local politics and in colonial government. Also, he used his cabinet influence to lobby for further increase in the legislative and in other arms of the colonial government. Such efforts began to bear fruit in 1960, when the traditional rulers were granted eight seats in the Legislative Council, their largest ever representation in the legislature. In addition, he was appointed minister of Works and Communication in the short lived coalition government assembled by Governor Edward Windley in May 1960. He was to retain this portfolio twice.

In March 1961, Mbacke was retained by P.S. Njie who had been asked to form a cabinet following the withdrawal of the PPP from the so-called Windley- Njie-Smith government. A year later, Mbacke was again invited into cabinet by D.K. Jawara whose party won the crucial elections of

1962. Following lengthy consultations with his constituency (chiefs) they accepted the communication minister's job in the new PPP cabinet.

Whilst in office, much improvement was registered in the communications sector in The Gambia. For instance the Brumen Bridge was rebuilt in 1962, a new ferry terminal was completed at Barra and national wireless service introduced with the commissioning of Radio Gambia in May 1962.

Chief Omar Mbacke's political activities were not restricted to Legislative and cabinet functions. For instance, he attended the 1961 Gambia Constitutional Talks called to "work out arrangements that will... Provide Gambia with a fully representative government as the only representative for the chiefs. During the Talks held in London, he spoke in favour of a gradual move towards independence in consideration of the country's weak economy. Of course the chief, like his colleagues, feared losing political clout to an independent government. He was, again, an active participant in the second Gambia Constitutional Talks held in London July 1964 when a date was agreed upon for Gambia's independence. However, the July Talk was to be among the last official functions of the chief as cabinet minister. A few weeks after his return home, Mbacke was dismissed from cabinet. Although no reasons were given publicly for the removal, it could have been due to his opposition to plans hatched by Premier Jawara and the other cabinet members to dispend with the services of a dozen chiefs, most of whom were suspected opposition sympathisers.

Out of the cabinet, Chief Omar Mbacke returned to Sami district and reclaimed the chieftaincy stool after an absence of four years. He had become chief of Sami in 1949 following the death of his father and was instrumental in the development of education in his district. He was responsible for the establishment of the school at Karantaba, and also encouraged his constituents to educate their wards.

Chief Omar Mbacke's interest in the development of education in the protectorate reflected his own colourful academic career as a student and teacher. He was educated at Armitage School in the mid-1940s and preceded to Sierra Leone where he trained as a Science teacher, returning home in 1945 to join the staff of his Alma matter. He helped to mould many Gambians who later served in senior government positions.

As one of the very few literate chiefs in the colonial era, Chief Omar Mbacke was the convener of several historic Chiefs' conferences between 1951 and 1960. He was the brain behind the historic 1959 Chiefs' conference held at Basse during which the traditional rulers gave their thumbs up for the establishment of the Protectorate People's Party meant to champion the rights and welfare of the protectorate peoples. He also convened the 1958 conference held at Brikama which sought to bridge the gap between the Bathurst politicians and the protectorate representatives.

Mbacke's illustrious career as a public servant was to come to an unceremonious end soon after the attainment of independence, to whose achievement he contributed a great deal. For in March 1965, he was among several chiefs sacked or retired. Unsuccessfully, he attempted several political comebacks by contesting the election in 1966 and in 1972.

Chief Omar Mbacke died in August 1994, at his birth place, Kolikunda, near Georgetown (Janjanbureh) at the age of 72. He will be remembered as the chief "Kingmaker" in 1961 and 1962, when the support of his constituency, the chiefs, was crucial in enabling P.S. Njie and D.K. Jawara to form governments respectively.

Henry Madi (1913-1965): Merchant and Nationalist Politician

'With the passing of Henry Madi, the Gambia mourned the loss of one of her greatest sons', a eulogist wrote in a tribute to this pioneer of big business and commerce in Gambia. Madi was a large-hearted philanthropist, an avowed nationalist who wielded much political clout in the turbulent but interesting Gambian Pre-Independence politics.

His political career started in 1951 when he got elected into the Legislative Council as the first member to represent the Kombo St. Mary constituency[93].

These elections came about as a result of the 1951 Wyn Harris Constitution for the Gambia which

[93] See *West Africa Magazine*, 18 September 1965, for an obituary of Mr. Madi. See also Hassoum Ceesay, 'Two eminent Gambians', *Weekend Observer*, May 30 1997.

was an improvement on the Backworth Wright Constitution of 1947, as it increased elected Legislative Council members from one (E.F. Small) to three, two to be elected in Bathurst, one for the Kombos and another to be nominated. One of the elected members was to sit in the Executive Council.

During his tenure in the Legco, Mr. Henry Madi ceaselessly championed an increase in the political and economic rights of his constituents. He lobbied for more political representation of Kombo Saint Mary and the rest of the Protectorate in the Legislative Council, and for the establishment of an autonomous local authority to manage the taxes and oversee the socio-economic development of this constituency. It was largely due to his efforts that the nucleus for what later became the Kanifing Urban District Council was implanted in the early 1960s. As a result of his satisfactory performance in the Legco, Mr. Madi was appointed to the all-powerful Executive Council (execo) in the early 1950s where he served until 1960. According to

David Williams, editor of *West Africa* magazine, this appointment made Mr. Henry Madi "the only none-African in modern times to be elected by African electors" in Commonwealth West Africa.[94]

In addition to his political roles in the legislature and Executive Council, Mr. Henry Madi also actively participated in pre- Independence party politics. He was among the founders and patrons of the Protectorate People's Party (PPP) and he served in the PPP's central coordinating body and was instrumental in wooing the business and Lebanese communities into the party. Moreover, he actively participated in both the 1961 and 1964 Gambia Constitutional Talks held in London to map out a political future for the country. On both occasions, he was part of the PPP delegation. During these talks, Madi was a dependable adviser on economic and financial issues for the leader of the PPP delegation, Dawda Jawara.

---

[94] See, *West Africa* magazine, 18 September 1965.

Besides his colourful political career, Henry Madi was also an accomplished and astute businessperson. He inherited his father's business ventures in 1962 and successfully turned it into a sprawling commercial concern whose tentacles reached all the corners of the country. The S. Madi Limited had branches in river port towns like Kuntaur, Kaur, Basse and Georgetown, employing hundreds of Gambians.

Madi also spread his business undertakings to the United Kingdom; the firm had branches in Manchester and London. In fact, by the mid-1960s, S. Madi Limited was a huge business with stakes in the construction industry, import and export, commerce and groundnut milling. Additionally, Madi developed the Atlantic Hotel into "the first really, good hotel in British West Africa" and the country's earliest tourist facility. He dedicated much of his business fortunes to philanthropic work especially towards youth development. He sponsored students, youth organisations and sporting endeavours, including football.

Equally noteworthy was Madi's pioneering role in the establishment of the Gambia Oil Seed Marketing Board (GOMA) in 1948, to market the country's main cash crop, groundnut. Mr. Madi served in the GOMB board from 1948-1954 and was instrumental in the setting up of GOMB up-river groundnut milling centre at Kaur and Kuntaur.

Henry Madi was born in 1913 and attended the Roman Catholic Mission school in Bathurst and later went to study in Manchester University in the United Kingdom. He returned home in 1938 to work in the family business, and he lived up river for many years in the early 1940s. He died in September 1965, in London.

M.B Jones (1918-1992): Anti-Colonial Editor and Nationalist Politician

Melvin Benoni Jones aka M.B Jones, was a nationalist politician, journalist and editor who upon his death was described as 'the last of that breed of journalists who spearheaded the fight against colonial rule in the pages of their newspapers'. Like his mentor E.F Small, he combined crusading journalism with militant politics and trade unionism to challenge colonial rule. Jones inherited and edited Small's *Gambia Oulook* for many decades till the mid-1980s when poor health made it difficult for him to continue[95].

'Jones was uncompromising in his stand against colonial rule and wayward colonial officials. He never hesitated to expose and condemn White

[95] For a rare insight into the life of MB Jones, see 'Death of a Journalist', *The Gambia News and Report Monthly*, August 1992, p.34-35. See also 'Grey-Johnson, N. *The Story of The Gambian Newspaper*, Banjul, 2005.

colonial servants who abused their powers, racist or inept'[96]. In a celebrated case in 1959, he exposed in the front page of his paper, the inability of the European Harbour Master of Banjul Wharf, Mr. Anderson, to successfully dock the MV Bamenda Palm which sailed from Freetown. It took nearly a week to berth the boat causing tons of bananas to rot in her cargo. Jones asked for the removal of Anderson. In May 1958, while editing the *Vanguard* in Bathurst, he had written a story about a European dentist who hit an old woman causing her bodily harm. He reported: 'Victoria hospital was the scene of the brutal act by an expatriate dentist, Mr. Adam, on an elderly female patient. He hit her forcefully on the bridge of her nose… because she complained of excessive pain over a broken tooth left in the mouth by the dentist the day before'.[97] The dentist took Jones to court for libel in the now famous Dentist Adams case of

---

[96] See Ceesay, H. 'Melvile Benoni 'M.B' Jones' Oxford African American Studies Centre, 2014.

[97] See 'Fatou Ceesay Dies', *Gambia Outlook*, 1972, p.1. This article recounts the life of the woman at the centre of the controversy, Fatou Ceesay, who had just died in Bathurst.

1958, actually a landmark development in the fight for press freedom in this country. Chief Justice Wiseman, sitting without a jury, dismissed the case with cost, making Jones another press hero, while Adams was withdrawn to England. This case like the Finden-Dailey case of 1948, contributed to freedom of expression in The Gambia.

Jones' brave journalism continued into the post-independence era when his paper, then reduced to cyclostyled sheets due to dwindling finances provided a forum for alternative views on the Jawara regime. Indeed, it was his Outlook and Dixon Colley's *Nation* which were the mainstay of the free press during the first two decades after independence. He mentored many young reporters and writers such as D.A. Jawo who became a leading editor in the 1990s. In 1966 and 1984, Jones led the efforts to establish an umbrella association for Gambian journalists; the result of which was the Gambia Press Union, now the vanguard for press freedom in the country. He was always convinced of the power of the press to effect positive change. 'A fearless, outspoken, unbiased newspaper is not only a desideratum to a backward and underdeveloped nation, but an indispensable tool for progress' Jones once said.[98] Another pithy statement of his was:

> Indeed, a newspaper in The Gambia is unlikely to be silenced by censorship. But it can very easily be silenced by economic pressures, so it is essential for a paper to be bold enough to catch the attention of as wide a cross section of the population as possible, and not merely as a vehicle for cheap adverts. There can be no doubt that a regular newspaper is essential to The Gambia. It is important that opinion should be widely aired and that the voice of the public should be heard. Naturally enough, that is not the wish of the imperialist rulers.[99]

Such was his steely fervour for press freedom in his country.

---

[98] See *Vanguard*, 12 May 1959.
[99] 'Editorial', *Gambia Outlook*, 1960.

Moreover, to his credit, Jones combined active journalism with politics. He believed that the two complement one another and politicians need the media to put their message across to voters, while the press need to always keep politicians on their toes to make them accountable to the people. Together with Bathurst accountant Kebba Wally Foon, he founded the National Party in 1958, which was the first political group to call for 'immediate' independence for the Gambia at a time the older parties were simply clamouring for self-government. This militancy endeared Jones and Foon to Nkrumah who invited them to attend the 1958 All African Peoples Conference. When the National Party was submerged into the United Party (UP), Jones contested the 1960 elections on a UP ticket, and retained his seat in 1962 for the Soldier Town constituency. Jones remained in parliament till 1966 when he lost his seat, an apparent victim of his own miscalculation in defecting to the Peoples Progressive Party (PPP), which had negligible support in Bathurst. He will be remembered as a skilled debater, who spoke against the flamboyance of the new independence leaders. 'Independence is not a piece of meat to be shared among hungry souls', he told MPs in the House. With Sir Dawda Jawara, he attended the Gambia's formal admission into the UN in September 1965, and was for many years President of the Gambia United Nations Association. MB Jones died in 1992 and was widely mourned as an indefatigable fighter of the right to free speech during and after colonial rule.

George St. Claire Joof (1908-1955): Lawyer and Political Leader

Joof was a lawyer, nationalist politician and theoretician. He was born in Bathurst in 1908; his father was J.P Joof, and mother Hannah Joof, both were teachers at the Dobson Street School during the 1890s. Straight from Dobson Street School, the young Joof entered the prestigious Methodist Boys' High School, where he won plaudits for his academic excellence and debating skills. In 1928, he entered Government service as clerk in the law courts where his passion for law grew by leaps and bounds. In 1945, he left Bathurst to study law in the UK and returned a qualified lawyer in February 1952. He returned to the government courts as a Prosecutor and in September 1952 acted as Attorney General and swore in Acting Governor Waddel while Governor Harris was on holiday[100]. He entered private practice and ran one of Bathurst

[100] See *Gambia Echo*, 18 September 1952, p.4.

most successful law firms. Soon Joof's firm was in the league of other great Bathurst lawyers like P.S Njie, Sam Forster, and E.D Njie.

In 1941, he married Lucretia St. Claire Joof with whom he travelled to the UK and was a source of inspiration to him during his studies. Lucretia St. Claire Joof was born in Banjul in 1913 and attended St Mary's Primary School and later the Methodist Girls' High School where she returned to teach in the early 1930s. Lucretia excelled as an educationist, merchant, nutritionist, politician, and a tireless advocate of women's emancipation. In 1968, she entered parliament as The Gambia's first woman MP. Her historic nomination by Prime Minister Dawda K. Jawara followed the passing of a bill in August 1968 to increase the number of nominated members of the House of Representatives from two to four 'so as to give more places to women'.[101] She was indeed a trailblazer as those were the days when it was still strange to hear women voicing their opinion in

---

[101] See *Gambia News Bulletin*, August 1968, p.1

public. 'My appointment shows the increasingly important role women are playing and will continue to play in the affairs of the country', she told reporters soon after her entry into parliament. When she left parliament in 1977, she continued to serve as a councillor at the B.C.C and re-introduced the council's funeral van service. She was a pillar in the political life of her husband who formed one of the earliest political parties in the Gambia.

George's Peoples' Party formed in 1953 and soon attracted many supporters convinced by the young politician's lucid statements and sound manifesto. Although a Methodist, Joof's support cut across the whole of Bathurst society, not the least because he had solid blood ties with famous Bathurst Muslims families like that of Madam Jilcock Loum, mother of the famous Muslim scholar Abdoulie Jobe.[102]

The 1954 elections, in which Joof contested as leader of his People's Party, deserve our closer

[102] See *Gambia Echo* Sept 27 19 54

attention for they were in many ways ground breaking in that they were contested under a party system, and were among the most hotly contested among all the previous elections held in the Colony. To start with, the elections were held under the new 1954 Constitution which was enacted in August 1954 and which provided among others the appointment of a Speaker for the Legislative Council, which was to be enlarged to 16 members, appointment of the first Gambian ministers, and the holding of party-based elections in the colony. Four political parties contested the three seats in Bathurst: P.S Njie's United Party, Garba Jahumpa's Muslim Congress, J.C Faye's Democratic Party and St. Claire Joof's Peoples' Party, while two Independents; John Madi and S.J Oldfield, contested for the single Kombo seat. For months preceding the October elections, Bathurst and the Kombo were gripped in election fever as the political parties actively canvassed for votes in public and private meetings. George St. Claire's favourite meeting place was the new Ritz Cinema where he addressed party supporters daily. In one such rally, he urged the large crowd to 'vote rightly and conscientiously, realizing that upon your vote depended the hopes of your future, the future of your children and future of your country'[103].

Joof's party manifesto was centred on winning internal self-government immediately as a prelude to full independence, promotion of girls' education and bridging the Colony-Protectorate divide. He faced a tough challenge from much more experienced political heavyweights like J.C Faye and Garba Jahumpa, whose parties were in existence for over five years and therefore had a solid basis of support. He attracted supporters from across the religious and generational divide. Joof's membership of the Reform Club enabled him to win the support of Aku professionals, intellectuals and younger voters. However, like other Bathurst politicians of his time, he failed to make any inroads into the Protectorate, therefore unable to widen his political support base beyond Bathurst.

---

[103] See *Gambia Echo*, 19 October 1953, p.10.

His sudden death in March 1955 brought untold grief and shock among his supporters, clients and the Bathurst community.

John Colley Faye (1909-1985): Religious Leader and Nationalist Politician

Reverend JC Faye was a religious leader, diplomat, cabinet minister, educationist, and pioneer politician whose contribution to the political and social development of The Gambia is immeasurable.[104]

Reverend Faye entered politics and founded The Gambia Democratic Party (GDP), the first political party in The Gambia, in 1951[105]. In 1952, JC Faye was elected first member for Bathurst and was appointed to cabinet as minister of Works and

[104] For an excellent account of Rev. J. C Faye's life, see Senghor, J. *The Reverend John Colley Faye: His Life and Times,* Author House, 2013, This is the first full length biograpgy of Faye, and of any Gambian leader.

[105] See Hughes, A. and David Perfect. 'Trade Unionism-The Gambia, *Journal of African Affairs*, 1989, P.351. For an interesting peep into Faye's later life see, Jay Saidy, 'Rev. J.C. Faye re-tyres' , *Gambia News Bulletin*, 7 October 1981, p.4.

Communications[106]. He served in that post until 1954, when his party contested the elections and he was re-elected into the Legislative Council. His Party manifesto for that election pledged to work for internal self-government for The Gambia, bring people of the Colony and Protectorate closer, tackle youth unemployment and widen access to health facilities in the country. He also sought to encourage Africanisation of the civil service by upgrading Gambian civil servants and enlarging their access to scholarships for further training, and to introduce new cash crops in the country such as sesame and cashew.

Faye's term in cabinet was a big success. In his tenure, work in the Trans-Gambia road, The Brumen Bridge, the Half-Die power plant and the West Africa Airways Corporation offices in Bathurst were all completed. Faye's Democratic party "spearheaded all constitutional changes in The Gambia" from 1951 to 1960. For example, he was instrumental in the formation of the All Party

---

[106] See *Gambia Echo*, 25 February 1952, p.1.

Committee under the chair of Henry Madi and the Committee of Citizens chaired by Ousman Jeng. Both committees submitted constitutional proposals to the people at mass meetings for ratification before forwarding them to the Secretary of State for the Colonies in 1959. These proposals formed the basis for the 1960 Constitution which introduced universal adult suffrage in the country. As Party leader of the Gambia Democratic Party, he attended the 1961 Gambian Constitutional Talks in London.

Following the 1962 elections, Faye again lost his Bathurst seat, but as he was in electoral alliance with the PPP, he was nominated by Government to represent The Gambia at the Court of St James, London, as Gambian Commissioner from 1963-64. He resigned over disagreement with the PPP's desire to turn The Gambia into a Republic after independence.

Reverend Faye was a consummate Pan Africanist. According to research done by AE Cham-Joof,

Faye, in 1954, issued a manifesto calling for a Federation of British West African colonies and a regional High Command. This was why he befriended great African leaders like Azikwe who invited him to attend his investiture ceremony as Governor General of Nigeria in 1960.

As an educationist, Reverend J.C Faye was a teacher and later headmaster of St Mary's School, Banjul. He opened the Kristikunda School in Kartora, Upper River Division, once called 'The Gambia's Achimota' for it produced prominent Gambian leaders of later years.[107] Therefore, Faye opened the gates of education to the provincial people. Some of his pupils later became important personalities in Gambian politics.

It was in recognition of his selfless services at Kristikunda that he was nominated a member of the prestigious Executive Council in 1947[108]. Reverend Faye has been described by a leading

---

[107] See 'Ceesay, H. 'John Colley Faye' Oxford African American Centre, 2014.

[108] See Hughes and Perfect, *Historical Dictionary*, p.61

Gambian historian the late A.E Cham-Joof, as the "architect" of tourism in The Gambia. As Gambian Commissioner to the UK, he encouraged the Lyndhurst Brothers to build the Adonis hotel which became the first tourist hotel in The Gambia.

Faye was an active church goer, a provost of the Anglican Church and a champion of the Wolof language. He wrote essays on Wolof syntax and formed an association to preserve the language. In recognition of his services to The Gambia, Reverend Faye was awarded Order of The Republic of The Gambia by President Jawara, a long-time political rival. He died in 1985.

Sanjally Bojang (1909-1995): Founder of the PPP and a Master Farmer

During his heyday as a labour contractor, Sanjally Bojang was one of the most known protectorate people living in Banjul. As a result, he became a pillar of hope around which the activities of the protectorate workers revolved. Bojang's involvement in politics began with a curious start. At that time patients from the protectorate who died at the Royal Victoria Hospital did not have proper Muslim funerary rites. Deceased Muslims were "mechanically" interred by the undertaker, Pa Dodgen. This issue aroused the interest of the then hospital administrator, Dr. S.H.O. Jones, who recognised Bojang's standing, approached him and prevailed on him to form an association to assist in the decent burial of protectorate deceased. With the help of one Mafoday Sonko, Bojang founded the Kombo Niumi Friendship Society[109].

[109] See 'Sanjally Bojang Dies' Sheriff Bojang, *Weekend Observer*, October 27, 1995 p.12, and subsequent articles

Three months later, this society's name was change to Lilahi wa Rasuli (For God and His Messenger) society, to attract broader support. Most of the corpses the society treated occurred at the Campama Mental Home and at the Mile Two Prisons.

Soon after the establishment of this society, political activity was allowed to distend into the hinterland. A meeting of the thirty -five chiefs was called in Brikama, and Sanjally and his society were given the green light to form a party on behalf of the protectorate people, However, recalled Bojang in an interview he gave to noted journalist Sheriff Bojang , the chiefs agreed that the rule of *Nyo fuu kalaaama*- a Mandinka term, meaning 'eat and pass the calabash round' should apply to Gambian politics. He meant that for too long politics had become the preserve of Bathurst

---

by AE Cham Joof paying tribute to Sanjally upon his death, in the *Daily Observer*. See also numerous interviews on Bojang in *Daily Observer* by Sheriff Bojang.

people and it was fair that the rest of the country also shared in the activity.

The chiefs' mandate was communicated to the Society in Bathurst, and a delegation went to inform the governor of their desire in setting up a protectorate political organization. However, the governor was unimpressed and it was only after much pressure that he agreed to give them the okay on the condition that they were able to organise a meeting within Banjul, which can attract even "a handful of people".

Sanjally Bojang continued to tell interviewer Sheriff Bojang:

> Seven days after the meeting with governor, on a breezy Sunday afternoon, the Lilahi wa Rasuli society held its inaugural meeting, the venue was Albion Place, and Bojang , who had just come from his dockyard, was the only speaker. His shirt covered with groundnut shell fritters.

> Bojang, standing on top of an empty oil drum (because no table was at hand) delivered what is recorded in Gambia political history as the "Albion place Declaration". Despite the scoffing and bantering from some curious Bathurst onlookers and despite its lack of a shapely organization, the society's Albion Place rally was a success beyond expectation. The governor got the news beforehand, and my people called on him and they were treated to coffee for the first time at Government House. License was granted and with that over, the focus of the protectorate people's battle was shifted.

To finance the new organization, Bojang withdrew his deposit balance at the Standard Bank, much to the chagrin of the manager, Mr. Miller, whose told , "you get luck, but you no get sense." He recruited young and educated protectorate men such as Dawda Jawara, Sheriff Sisay and Sheriff Dibba to lead the new organisation which soon metamorphosed into the Protectorate Peoples' Party (PPP).

Blue, symbolising the tranquillity of the deep ocean, was adopted as the colour of the new party. To set the ball rolling, two campaign teams were set up to ply the north and south banks respectively. The teams met a lot of stiff resistance from some of the chiefs, some of whom could not bear the sight of choosing Jawara 'leather-tanner' over their sons. However, these oppositions were neutralised mainly due to Bojang 's bluffing tactics. In the ensuing year, Bojang's relationship with the Protectorate People Party, which was later changed to the Peoples' Progressive party, became a controversial affair, and Bojang was expelled from the party in 1961 when he tried to form an alliance with the UP of P.S Njie behind the back of the party leader. After the 1960 general elections, Bojang had invited all the leaders of the main political parties in The Gambia at a meeting at the Bathurst Town Council (BTC) chambers in Clifton Road to discuss forming a united front. This was with a view to demanding Self-Government from the colonial administration. Jawara, the PPP leader, sensed victory at the next polls and was opposed to this idea. Jawara had the party leadership expel its founder, Sanjally Bojang. This was the first internal crises to rock the PPP, and the start of a series of purges of party adherents whom Jawara suspected of being a threat to his leadership.

Following this expulsion and his failed attempt to form a new party called the Solidarity Party, Bojang decided to retire and to concentrate on farming. First, he rehabilitated Kembuje and started on horticultural production. He settled in Kembuje in the 1962-63 crop seasons. After spending a few years at Kembuje, he founded the 500-acre-farm at Nianibere.

His first priority was to go in for the growing of confectionery nuts (HPS), locally known as *Brukuss*, and was later appointed sole buying agent for the buying of this type of groundnuts on behalf of the GOMB. He pioneered the exportation of vegetables to Europe. Sanjally died in 1995 at Kembuje, near Brikama.

Alhaji I.M Garba Jahumpa (1909-1994): Nationalist Politician

Alhaji Jahumpa was a man of varied vocations. He excelled as a teacher, school administrator, trade unionist and most notably a nationalist politician who had a brilliant career which lasted for over half a century.

Jahumpa entered mainstream Gambian politics in 1951 when he established The Gambia Muslim Congress (GMC) which was the first recognized political party in the country. He formed the party soon after the promulgation of the 1951 constitution, which had provided for sweeping political reforms in response to agitations for more political emancipation spearheaded by E.F. Small, Sir John Mahoney and other militants of the independent (Gambia) National Congress of British West Africa (NCBWA). Jahumpa's party, like the

NCBWA, aimed for the gradual emancipation of The Gambia and the eventual realisation of a United Africa. To meet its goal, the Muslim Congress put up its leader to contest the legislative elections of 1951. Jahumpa won one of two Bathurst seats and opened for himself a new career in Gambian politics.

Further constitutional amendments in 1954 led to fresh elections on political party basis for the four elected legislative seats in the colony and for the appointment of Gambians to the executive council. The Gambia Muslim Congress sponsored Jahumpha who retained his Bathurst seat. Jahumpa was nominated to the Executive Council, as minister of Agriculture making him one of three Gambians to enter the cabinet of the colonial government.

Besides its historic significance, this nomination of Gambians into the Executive Council also marked the end of colonial rule in The Gambia. Gambians began to have the authority to make decisions affecting the lives of their compatriots at the high cabinet level and also acquired leadership experience. Jahumpha stayed in cabinet till 1960 when he lost his half-die ward in The Gambia's first General Elections under universal adult suffrage. His defeat by the UP candidate J.H. Joof was indeed a severe blow to the political fortunes of Jahumpha but it fell short of making Jahumpha a political featherweight for a year later, he attended the Constitutional Talks in London convened to map out further constitutional progress for The Gambia. As a representative of one of the three existing political parties, Jahumpha supported calls for fresh election to elect a government, which would guide the country to full independence at the shortest possible time. The delegates were finally all agreed on fresh elections and they were pencilled for May 1962.

Jahumpa contested the 1962 elections on this ticket of his Gambia Congress Party for the half-die ward. Again, he lost to his rival by the smallest of all margins, just eleven votes. His defeat was also the most surprising for he organised an elaborate campaign which included party radio broadcasts and live entertainment by music bands.

The most notable of such music groups was The Ramblers sent from Ghana by Dr. Kwame Nkrumah to help raise funds for Jahumpha and his party in their election campaign. This was one of many manifestations of the close ties between the Gambian politician and the Ghanaian leader. These ties were knotted as early as 1945 when Jahumpa met Nkrumah at the Pan African meeting in Manchester, England. Jahumpa, who represented The Gambia, was highly enamoured to the socialist and Pan-Africanist ideas of the Osagyefo and henceforth took up Nkrumah's political radicalism, socialism and African unity.

Jahumpa used the pages of his party newspaper, appropriately named AFRICAN UNITY, to call for the political and economic unification of Africa. In 1960, he campaigned on the platform to taking an independent Gambia into the folds of the ultraradical Pan-Africanist Casablanca Group which consisted of Ghana, Mali, Guinea and other socialist oriented African countries.[110]

In fact, Jahumpa was also a socialist during the early 1960s. Besides his closeness to Kwame Nkrumah, he also frequently visited countries in the socialist bloc, such as China and Russia. In 1968, Jahumpa completed a month long tour of these countries and later spoke highly of their socio-economic strides. In addition, Jahumpa attended seminars at the bastion of African Socialism, the Winneba Ideological Institute in Ghana. His inclination towards socialism made him the earliest politician to espouse radical politics as a means for achieving the socio-economic development of The Gambia. In 1962, a leading *West Africa* magazine described Jahumpa as "the most politically astute" of Gambian politicians, an accolade he really deserved as a result of various well calculated and pragmatic

[110] See *West Africa* Magazine, 21 February 1962.

political decisions he made during his political career.

Perhaps, Jahumpa's earliest show of political pragmatism occurred in 1960, when he and J.C. Faye sealed the first political party alliance in Gambian history. In an attempt to neutralise the UP threat in the colony, Jahumpa wooed Rev. J.C. Faye to ally with his Gambia Congress Party forming the Democratic Congress Alliance (DCA). The DCA contested the 1960 elections but lost heavily and it was dissolved in 1961. In 1962, Jahumpa allied with the PPP but again lost the elections and only re-entered parliament in 1966 paving the way for the most pragmatic move in his political career: joining the PPP in March 1968, after the dissolution of his Congress Party. This historic decision was the result of several months of negotiations between the two parties at the end of which a joint communiqué issued by the parties indicated that the "GCP and PPP have agreed to merge into a single party to be known as the PPP". Later, Jahumpa declared: "We joined the PPP unconditionally, unreservedly and not seeking office" and "for the sake of national unity".[111]

The merger benefited both parties. It helped PPP to win its first seat in Bathurst in1972 and also Jahumpa was made Minister of Health in April 1968.

As Health Minister, Jahumpa negotiated The Gambia's entry into World Health Organisation in 1971 and the inauguration of several health facilities countrywide. He was Minister of Finance from 1972 to 1977.

[111] See *Gambia News Bulletin*, March 1968, p.1

Assan Musa Camara (1923-2013): Politician

Assan Musa Camara was born in Mansanjang, Basse, URD in 1923[112]. His father was a prominent farmer and Cattle breeder. He attended St. Mary's Catholic Mission School, Bathurst between 1930-38. During the years 1938-48, Camara attended the Catholic mission school Kristi Kunda in the Kantora District, URD. There he was converted to the Anglican Church and took the name Andrews. He taught at Kristikunda, for twelve years from 1948. Kristikunda became the training ground for many future Gambian leaders who passed through his hands, which later became an asset to his political career.

He contested The Gambia's first general elections in 1960 on the UP ticket. He won the Kantora seat

---

[112] See, Hughes and Perfect, *Historical Dictionary*, p.29, 30.

and joined the Unity Government as Minister of Health. When this government collapsed in 1961, he remained to serve in PS Njie's cabinet. He retained his seat in the 1962 general elections.

In 1963, Camara cross carpeted to the PPP and was made Minister for Education and Social Welfare replacing another Fula politician Paul Baldeh who died in 1968. In fact, Baldeh's declining fortunes in the PPP was largely as a result of Camara's entry into the party.

Camara soon became a close confidante of Sir Dawda. Camara served in the cabinet continuously in various capacities from 1963- 1982 becoming The Gambia's leading Fula politician.

Camara served as Vice President from 1972 –1977 and from 1978-82 as foreign minister, from 1968 - 1977, Camara forged Gambia's Foreign policy, particularly relations with Senegal and the communist Block. In October 1973, Camara visited North Korea that led to the establishment of diplomatic relations with Pyongyang. It was largely as a result of his influence that The Gambia became the first African country to recognise Guinea Bissau's independence in 1973.

It was largely due to Camara's intervention that the 1981 coup attempt failed. From his hiding at the Chinese Embassy in Banjul, he was in constant contact with President Jawara who was trapped in London. This was critical in the intervention of the Senegalese troops to quell the coup.

However, despite retaining his seat in Parliament in 1982, he was dropped from the cabinet. Following a few years sitting in the backbenches, he left the party in 1986 to form the Gambia's Peoples' Party (GPP). Despite a brief flourish, the party did badly in the 1987 elections. Allegations of sponsorship by foreign business tycoons and the arrest of some of the party's top members undermined the GPPs credibility. Camara failed to regain his seat in parliament in the 1992 elections and his political career continued to wane. He died in December 2013.

Eric Herbert Christensen (1923-1990): Career Civil Servant

In his compendious essay, "From Green Revolution to National reconciliation: The PPP in the Gambia 1959- 1973", Arnold Hughes, a leading scholar on Gambian politics footnoted that Eric Herbert Christensen was among the three "most influential men" in the Gambia. In an article in his "Roots" series, Jay Saidy described Christensen as one of the most powerful men in the Gambia of the 1970s, a scholar and voracious reader; whilst C.A. Jallow wrote that Christensen was a "self- made man'[113]. Indeed these are fitting accolades for Christensen, considering the numerous positions of trust and clout he held. Whilst being in the Civil Service from 1965 to 1978, and his spectacular rise through

[113] See *Gambia Weekly*, 3 August 1990, p.9 for a short tribute published upon his death. See also, 'Notable Gambians' Hassoum Ceesay *Weekend Observer*, July 25 1997, p.11.

the ranks of the Service to become Secretary General to the government in 1970.

Christensen joined the independent Gambia Civil Service in 1965 as Assistant Secretary at the Ministry of External Affairs, and by virtue of hard work and experience he was quickly promoted to Principal Assistant Secretary at the Prime Minister's office in 1966. Later that year, he was appointed permanent secretary at the Prime Minister's office, External Affairs as well as Secretary to the Cabinet concurrently. At the External Affairs ministry, he helped to nurture a non-aligned, cost effective foreign policy by opening diplomatic missions in only a few select places like Dakar, London and New York. This far-sighted move saved the Gambia from the pitfall of cumbersome diplomatic missions which other independent states like Ghana had fallen into.

In 1967, the post of Head of the Civil Service was added to his responsibilities and here he was keen in quickening the pace of Gambianisation of the

Public Service. In late 1967, he was appointed head of Gambian diplomatic missions.

To crown his numerous portfolios, Eric was appointed the Gambia's first Secretary General, Office of the President in 1970, making him a close confidant of Sir Dawda Jawara. This became the most powerful post in the Civil Service, and Christensen was charged with the task of formulating policies to meet The Gambia's development needs and he largely succeeded in this by assembling a strong team of technocrats such as Dr. Jabez Ayo Langley, long time Permanent Secretary at the Ministry of Economic Planning; T.G.G. Senghore, Permanent Secretary of Finance; Dr Lamin Mbye, Director of Information Services and S.M Sissoho, Permanent Secretary at Works, among others. Christensen brought efficiency to the service, and by the time he retired in late 1978, The Gambia Civil Service was the best run in former British West African colonies.

It is important to highlight the salient role of The civil service in the first fifteen years after Independence, as the catalyst for social and economic development. Up till 1982, the majority of Jawara's cabinet were barely literate politicians who though loyal to Jawara and committed, lacked the technical largesse to run the country which is why Civil Servants had to bear the burden of defining, refining and executing policies. Thus they were also very powerful, independent and highly respected by the political class. The fact that Christensen stoutly and jealously defended the neutrality of Civil Servants also added to their prestige in the first fifteen years after independence.

He was the force behind the commissioning and adoption of the Nti report, which recommended a large increase in civil servant remunerations and benefits. Also, Christensen was happily involved in the government's attempts to cash in on the publication of the novel "Roots" to boost tourism and investment in The Gambia by approving the dispatch of a team of Gambians to publicise it in the United States.

Christensen's colourful civil service career after independence was facilitated by the reservoir of experience he had before 1965 as a teacher at Saint Augustine's Secondary from 1941 to 1943, member of the West African Army crops 1943 to 1945 and as consul at the Senegalese consulate in Banjul from 1961 to 1965 when he actively supported closer ties between The Gambia and Senegal.

A discussion of his life should afford us the opportunity to touch briefly on the process of Gambianisation of the Civil Service from 1962 to 1970, when it was the expressed policy of the PPP government to elevate Gambians to Civil Service jobs formerly held by Europeans. This policy was the logical follow up to the earlier policy of Africanisation started under the administration of Governor Backworth Wright in 1946 to Africanise the Civil Service and European firms. Gambianisation started in 1962 and by 1966, key

Government departments like Accountant General's chambers, Customs, Printing, Labour, Lands, and Surveys were led by Gambians and had a wholly Gambian staff. In addition, there were 13 Gambians out of the 21 key administrative officials mandated with efficient execution of ministerial policies of Government. To facilitate the process of Gambianisation, the Public Service Commission formed in 1952 was enlarged and added new responsibilities of providing training for young Gambians to enable them to occupy positions of responsibilities in government. Through this policy, young administrators such as D.A Ndow, F.A.J. Savage, H.R Monday Jr., M.M Sosseh, and Dr Jabez Langely amongst others, rose steadily to become seasoned and competent administrators who took over from departing British experts such as K.J.W. Lane, D.A Percival and H.A Oliver.

The policy of Gambianisation was one of the early success stories of the PPP government in the early 1960s. Christensen as Head of civil service played a key role in the success of this policy and helped to build the Gambian Civil Service which became renowned as the most efficient in the Commonwealth. Sadly, a heavy cloud loomed over the Civil Service caused by a number of reasons including; mass retrenchment in the 1980s, the increasing political interference in the work of the Gambian Civil Service and in it's appointments, the rise of the private sector in the 1990s, and the 1981 coup attempt. The Civil Service has not been able to recover its glory days.

Christensen was a scholar of repute. He read widely and in 1954 translated, from Portuguese into English, the 1570 account of a Portuguese sailor who visited the Gambia. This book, serialized in The Gambia Echo from May 1954, was the first full insight of the conditions of the country in the 16th century.

Christensen was a deeply private man and this added to the aura of seriousness and impartiality which surrounded him throughout his illustrious career as Head of The Gambian Civil Service[114]. Christensen died in Canada in 1990.[115]

---

[114] Interview with retired Gambian Permanent Secretary and diplomat, and former colleague of him, January 2011.

[115] See also M. F Singhateh, 'A Supreme Administrator' *Topic Magazine*, August 1990, p. 25 for an appreciation of Christensen's life following his demise written by a seasoned Gambian civil servant.

M.E Jallow (1923-1987): Trade Union Leader

In a 1961 profile, the authoritative *West Africa* magazine described ME Jallow, the leader of the Gambia Workers' Union (GWU), as the "most powerful man in the Gambia". At the time, this was even an understatement; ME's political, economic and labour clout was so huge, so strong that he ought to as well have been called the only powerful man in the colony. M.E Jallow was a consummate trade unionist, a feisty politician, and an uncompromising crusader for social justice whose rise to fame and influence was deeply rooted in his educational and occupational career.

Jallow was born in June 1928, Georgetown, CRD. In 1939, he moved to Bathurst and attended St Augustine's School where he graduated in 1950 with a Cambridge School Leaving Certificate. He worked at the education department as a clerk till 1954 when he went to Ibadan, Nigeria, to study cooperative management. He returned in 1956, and was appointed to the newly created post of cooperative animator in which position he familiarised himself with the membership of small scale cooperative societies such as those of artisans, construction workers and dockers.

Jallow was so appalled by the working condition of certain sectors of the labour force he had encountered that he resigned from the Civil Service in late 1956, and established the GWU to challenge the colonial government's labour policies.

The formation of the GWU was indeed timely. Then, the only major trade union was the moribund Gambia Labour Union, (GLU) formed by EF Small in 1929, but as Small was in frail health, the GLU had become fragmented in the early 1950s and lacked effective leadership and focus.

Jallow succeeded quickly in strengthening the GWU through a massive membership recruitment drive. Unlike other trade unions, who recruited their members mainly from skilled labour such as clerks, Jallow wooed mainly unskilled labour such as dock workers.

A leading labour historian, David Perfect, explained in his profound thesis 'Labour and Politics in the Gambia, 1900- 1984', that "M.E Jallow targeted those unskilled workers whose working conditions were atrocious enough to be ignited at any time." Jallow's efforts yielded results as the GWU membership swelled to several hundred within its first year of existence. Another reason for the GWU success was Jallow's Midas touch; his inimitable ability to win concessions such as pay rises for workers which made many workers to flock to the Union.

For example, in 1953, he was called upon by GWU members working at the Gambia Minerals Ltd's illeminite mines at Brufut, to help them get a pay rise. Jallow successfully got a pay rise from the all-European management, even though the mines closed soon after in 1958. Also, in 1957, Jallow secured a pay rise for workers of the Gambia Construction Company Ltd.

Foreign assistance also contributed to Jallow's success as a trade unionist. In 1959, he got a $5,000 grant from the Ghana government, and another fifty thousand francs from the government of the newly independent Guinea led by Ahmed Sekou Toure. Jallow also benefitted from training in Uganda under an International Confederation of Free Trade Unions (ICFTU) scholarship in 1958. Such funding and training not only gave the GWU a sound financial base, a prerequisite for successful activities, but also helped Jallow to varnish his leadership qualities.

Jallow's canny strike tactics were legendary, and also accounted for the phenomenal success of the GWU as a trade union. He was so calculating that he only organised strikes at the worst possible moment for the employers. In 1959, dock workers wanted a pay rise but negotiations were hard and unmoving. Jallow led the workers into strike minutes after an ocean liner belonging to Elder Dempster Shipping Lines vessel carrying perishables like tomatoes and beef had docked at Banjul port. The ports authority quickly accepted a 12.5 per cent wage rise for the dockers who went back to work with haste. In 1960, Jallow organised another strike by cooperative workers at the peak of the groundnut trade season when their services were most crucial. Again, the workers carried the day.

Jallow's real test as a labour leader, however, was the 1960 and 1961 strikes which he successfully led. The 1960 strike by the Gambia Workers' Union was called to expedite an increase in the minimum wage and for recognition of the Union by the colonial government. On February 2nd 1960, Jallow led a huge crowd of protesting workers and other dissatisfied young Gambians through the streets of Bathurst. The crowd sang anti-colonial songs and displayed pro-independence banners. The government was so rattled by the demonstration that it ordered the police to break it up.

Although Jallow and his comrades were dispersed by police teargas and truncheons, they still carried on. A week after the strike, Governor Ed Windley agreed to the demands of the workers for a comprehensive review of the salary structure. The Panda Salary Review Commission formed as a result and recommended a fifteen per cent salary hike and that the minimum daily wage also hiked from four to five shillings. Another achievement of the strike was the formation of a labour board to recruit labourers for the docks chaired by the Director of Medical Services, Dr. S.H.O Jones. Hitherto, the recruitment of Dockers was a monopoly of Sanjally Bojang, later founder member of the PPP and Chief of Brikama, who discriminated against Bathurst Wollofs and Sereres in favour of his Mandinka mates.

Emboldened by his success, Jallow called another major strike in January 1961 to yet press for more wages. He led seven hundred angry marchers from the Marine department through all the major streets of Bathurst until police used teargas to disperse the crowd. As the strike persisted into its fifth day, Bathurst had grounded to a halt; the government had to again yield a thirteen per cent salary increase and agreed to the formation of a joint industrial council to arbitrate labour issues.

The 1961 strike catapulted Jallow into a national political figure, a true nationalist who dared to challenge the colonial establishment. Jallow told Perfect (1987) that the strike was not staged solely for wage increase, but to also press for 'independence'. Having clearly proven his political relevance, Jallow earned himself a place in both the Independence Talks of 1961 and 1964 in London where he stoutly asked for immediate independence for the country.

Strangely however, Jallow shunned mainstream Gambian political parties until 1966. He kept his distance from all the parties in the 1960 and 1962 elections insisting that he was a trade unionist. In 1961 he declined the invitation to join Sanjally Bojang's ephemeral Solidarity Party. In addition, Jallow must have found it hard to lay his support on any particular party as he was close to the leadership of both the United Party and the PPP. However, by late 1965, he was forced to re-consider his political non-alignment in the face of calculated attempts by the PPP regime to kill off the GWU.

Even before Independence, the PPP had become frightened of the ever growing GWU popularity and that of its undisputed leader, Jallow. Their fears laid in the fact that Jallow, too, hailed from the Protectorate and could, therefore, mount a serious challenge to the PPP's hegemonic grip of the provinces. Secondly, Jallow was more politically savvy than the lucky PPP upstarts. Above all, he had a ready arsenal of support in the

GWU membership which at the time was the most organized body in the Gambia.

The PPP's first assault on the GWU came in 1964 when it ordered massive retrenchment of workers at the Public Works Department (PWD), the reservoir of GWU support. The redundancies affected a third of PWD workers and knocked a hole in GWU support. The second assault came in 1965, when the PPP government encouraged one Henry Forster to form a rival labour body called the National farmers and General Workers Union. It was given furnished offices, cars and Forster was a regular guest to cocktails at No. 2 Marina, the official residence of the Prime Minister. Thus, Jallow opposed and campaigned against the 1965 Republican Referendum as he feared that President Jawara would destroy organised labour. The success of the NO vote in that referendum encouraged Jallow to seek political office as an Independent Candidate in the 1966 elections on the Bathurst North ticket. Jallow got only 125 votes, and this defeat ended his brief dalliances with party politics, and it cost him his legitimacy as a labour leader. Jallow opposed the 1970 Republican referendum. And when the YES won, he sank further into political insignificance. The PPP quickly deregistered the GWU under the pretext of financial mismanagement. Under the PPP, Jallow's GWU had become moribund and irrelevant.

In 1987, Jallow was nominated into parliament but he died before he took up his seat. He is remembered as the first and last influential labour leader in The Gambia after EF Small of the 1920s. Garba Jahumpa described him as 'the greatest labour leader of his time', upon his death on 26 May 1987.

Abdoulie Samba (1924-1980): Wollof Griot and Cultural Ambassador

Griots have long been respected for the power their music can carry. Although the role of the griot has diminished with the evolution of contemporary society and the passage of time, the griot still remains an integral part of the culture of Gambia and the strongest link to centuries of history. For centuries, court musicians and 'griots' (story-tellers) have kept alive tales of family and village history, and you may find them singing their oral accounts and stories accompanied by an instrument. Although the role of the griot has diminished with the evolution of contemporary society and the passage of time, the griot still remains an integral part of the culture of The Gambia and the strongest link to centuries of history. They sometimes belong to the household of a nobleman, appointed to sing the virtues of their benefactor and master. However, most are independent; singing the praises of anyone who can pay them and a less generous clientele might find the song more critical than giving praise. Because of their deep knowledge of history, they are often viewed with a mixture of fear and admiration.

When a griot dies, it is like a whole library is burnt down, and one such library was closed down with the demise in April 1980 of Alhaji Abdoulie Samba, master xalamist, bard and proponent of Wollof culture[116]. He was among the most famous exponents of Gambian culture in the 1960s through to his death in 1980, presenting cultural programmes in the new Radio Gambia, working in the first Gambia National Troupe, and participating in major tourism promotional tours of The Gambia around the world. Samba was above all one of the last classic Wollof bards (gewel) who lived by singing the praises and genealogies of their patrons.

---

[116] See *Gambia News Bulletin*, 15 April 1980, p.2.

He started his career in the retinue of the famous Badibu Chief Mama Tamba Jammeh in the 1940s, accompanying Tamba Jammeh in his numerous forays in the Protectorate explaining Government policy to the farmers as member of the Legislative Council. His sonorous voice and beautiful *xalam* tunes were the hallmark of Chief Tamba's visits to the major wharf towns such as Kaur, Belingho and Ballanghar.

After the end of the Second World War, the young griot moved to Bathurst to join the lively and highly influential groups of minstrels in the capital. The advent of party politics after the Second World War had made griots a much-needed pack to enlist voters and animate political rallies. J.C Faye, P.S Njie, Garba Jahumpa and other party leaders had their bands of griots who would not only sing their praises but also denigrate their opponents. These were boom times of the gewels. Samba quickly made a name for himself in Bathurst working closely with P.S Njie's United Party, composing numerous tunes extolling the virtues of the party and its leader.

Thus when Radio Gambia was opened in 1962 by P.S Njie, then Chief Minister, quickly got a spot in the new Radio's programme schedule hosting a popular weekly slot called *'Jamma Bahni chi reew'* (Peace helps build a nation). This was one of many programmes on the new station developed to unite Gambians whilst also reviving cultural practices and songs. His xalam tunes were soon adopted as the signature tunes for many Wollof programmes on the Radio including the noon news bulletins.

In 1974, Samba was part of the nucleus of artists tasked to form the first Gambia National Troupe. This was a time when the PPP Government, having won political independence, was keen to project the cultural image of the country to the outside world and to also attract tourists and investors. The National Troupe comprised performers from all the ethnic groups, and toured the country playing to packed audiences. In 1975, Samba led the Troupe to a tour of the USSR, and in 1976 took the Troupe to perform in Libya. As the Government was unable to post diplomats in friendly countries due to budgetary and manpower constraints, the troupe was engaged in cultural diplomacy to friendly countries far and near.

In 1977, Samba was a member of the Gambian contingent to the Second Festival of Black Arts held in Lagos, Nigeria, and later that summer, he was among the Gambian Cultural Mission to the USA and the Caribbean[117]. This mission was dispatched by Government to take advantage of the Roots euphoria stirred up by the publication in 1976, the book and film Roots by Alex Haley, which traces his ancestry to the Gambia. Government, propelled by the efficient and influential Secretary General Eric Christensen, needed to take the Roots message to the USA to sell Gambia as the land of Roots to

---

117 See 'Roots' by Jay Saidy, *Daily Observer*, May 7, 1997. Other members of this historic delegations were:Jay Saidy, Junaidi Jallow, Charles Thomas, B.K Sidibe, Fabala Kanuteh , Nurse Kanuteh, Musu Kebba Drammeh.

the huge African American community. The mission was also meant to help discredit press reports which were claiming that the Roots story was false. Above all the mission spreaded Gambian culture to the wider American public through their five weeks tour. The mission was a resounding success which put The Gambia firmly on the USA psyche and helped to attract visitors to the Gambia. Twenty years later in 1996, the Roots International Festival was created to rejuvenate the interest of the African Diaspora in the Roots saga. He died in Banjul in April 1980.

Sir Dawda Kairaba Jawara (1924-): First President of The Gambia

Unlike many African leaders of the first generation, very little is on record about the career of Sir Dawda Kairaba Jawara before 1959 when he helped form the PPP, the nationalist party which was to eventually take The Gambia into full nationhood in 1965. He was an anonymous civil servant, 'cow doctor' (as Professor Arnold Hughes calls him) in a small office somewhere in Abuko, 15 km outside Banjul, whom the press did not mention in their reports. So much of what we now know about Sir Dawda's early life was gleaned from his 2011 autobiography 'Kairaba'. And this part of Sir Dawda's life is of utmost importance to us historians because it laid the framework for his later life. To know the Jawara who ruled the Gambia from 1962 to 1994, we must know the young Jawara of Barajally Tenda, Muhameddan and Methodist Boys' High School (MBHS) in Bathurst, etc. It must be said that the ability of Jawara to set up a party with nothing except a few inexperienced provincials, no resources except the pecuniary goodwill of Sanjally Bojang and his own meagre savings, and win national elections within three years is an unmatched success in West African politics. Even Nkrumah spent five years building the CPP between his return from studies to winning the 1951 Ghana Elections. This dazzling party political success too could only be explained by Jawara's rural origins and his strong connections with eminent Bathurst families.

David Perfect in his magisterial *Historical Dictionary of The Gambia* tells us that Jawara was born in Barajally on 16 May 1924.[118] His father Almamy, was a 'prosperous' trader and farmer. The two roles were in most parts complementary in rural Gambia of the 1920s: during the rainy season, the

---

[118]See Hughes, A. and Perfect, David. *Historical Dictionary of The Gambia.* Scarecrow Press, 2008, p.113. In his autobiography, Jawara describes this date as 'the best estimate of my date of birth', See, Jawara, Sir Dawda. *Kairaba*, Domtom Publishing, 2009, p.1.

traders will close shop and till their fields; from November to June, the groundnuts trade season, they will return to the riverside towns called *tendas* to open their shops. Almamy was most likely a trader's agent than a merchant; the big trading houses in Bathurst such as Vezia, Palmine and Maurel et Freres, for example, usually employed agents in their upriver stations on commission during the trade season.

Jawara's father built a wide network of business friends, one of whom Pa Yoma Ebrima Jallow lived in Bathurst and one day while on a business trip to Walikunda, near Barajally, where Almamy had his shop, the young Jawara was entrusted to Ebrima who willingly took him to school in Bathurst.

The young Jawara quickly completed his primary school at Muhameddan and proceeded to the Methodist Boys High School where he graduated in 1945, aged 21. This was quite an old age for a High School pupil, which was why he did not waste much time in seeking college admission. In

1947, he won a scholarship to Achimota College in Ghana, a famous and highly regarded institution in British West Africa at the time. It was the incubator for many future leaders ranging from Nkrumah to Azikwe, both founding fathers of modern Ghana and Nigeria. From Achimota, he proceeded to study medicine at Edinburgh, Scotland. His two years stint at the Victoria Hospital in Bathurst and one year pre-university course at Achimota had put him in good stead in his medical course.

From 1954 to 1960, except for a year long absence to complete a diploma in tropical veterinary medicine, Jawara served as chief veterinary officer of the Gambia under the colonial administration. This was a high position in the civil service which ensured him a car and furnished official quarters. Already, Jawara was a senior official in the colonial hierarchy. However, this posed as much dissatisfaction as the comforts that came with the post. In most cases, such highly placed Africans such as Jawara became disgruntled because even if they were more qualified than their White peers, they still received less pay and were subjected to untold racial slurs. Jawara had protested over the colonial officials' disregard of his proposal for a salary upgrade for himself and his assistants.[119] When his White bosses refused to take action, he resigned his post. Now, even he admits in his autobiography that the salary dispute was merely the cause for his resignation; the reason was that certain notables from his Mandinka ethnic group had gone to see him to encourage him to lead a new political party they had formed so as to reverse the Bathurst domination of Gambian party politics at the time.

This party was called the Protectorate Peoples' Party (PPP), later called Peoples' Progressive Party. The party came out of the disaffection created by the collective anger of the protectorate educated elite who rightly felt that Bathurst had taken total control of the political life of the country even though it accounted for only twenty per cent of the country's population. Of the four political parties

---

[119] See *Kairaba*, p.194.

that were active in local politics in 1959, when the PPP was formed, all were led by Bathurst politicians and none had any base or structures outside the urban areas.[120] This was an era of political exclusion encouraged by the colonialists' divide and rule tactics, and made inevitable by the fact that almost all the possibly qualified people to lead active political life by virtue of educational attainment were in Bathurst as there were few educational opportunities open to people in the rural areas. At this time, there were only two Mandinkas who had attained university degrees- himself and Lamin Marenah. When the latter unequivocally rejected the offer of political leadership of the PPP, Jawara had to accept the call of his people. By his side he had a coterie of young high school Mandinka graduates such as S. M Dibba,[121] S.S Sisay [122] and Yaya Ceesay. [123]

---

[120] The parties were United Party (UP) led by P. S N'jie; Muclim Congress Party (MCP) led by Garba Jahumpa; National Party of K. W Foon; Democratic Party led by J.C Faye.

[121] S.M Dibba (1937-2008); he served as minister and vice president before leading the opposition against the PPP regime; and served as speaker of the National Assembly during the Second Republic.

At this time, it required strong will and undiluted intrepidness to engage in nationalist politics and therefore stand up to the colonial rulers. For Jawara, in particular, a senior government job with its perks was at stake. Thus it should be to his credit that he mustered the courage to plunge into the struggle to kick out colonial domination.

While he had the educational qualifications, he lacked the wherewithal to organise and mobilise around the country. Thus Sanjally Bojang, a rich Mandinka trader, came in handy to bankroll the party. By 1960, the party, only 14 months old, was able to win more seats in the rural areas than its rivals. For the PPP, the provinces have become a stronghold and for a while the party associated itself with the needs of the rural masses.

---

[122] S.S Sisay (1935-1989); he served as finance minister and later Governor of the Central Bank of The Gambia;
[123] Yaya Ceesay(1937-) served in PPP cabinets from 1962 to 1994.

When he led the PPP to victory in the 1962 elections, Jawara's nationalist credentials were no longer in doubt so was his political astuteness. He knew from his long association with sections of the Bathurst Krio and Wollof elite that a segment of this group did not subscribe to the domination by urban Wollof and Krio of all aspects of political life. He quickly tapped into this restive Bathurst niche and soon the PPP was no longer a Protectorate's Peoples' Party; it had become national in hue and composition. In 1962, he had a notable Bathurst Wollof politician, A.B N'jie, in his first cabinet.

Jawara also was skilful in his handling of the departing British. He did not stampede them into packing as Nkrumah did in Ghana; nor did he antagonise them. He maintained warm relations with Whitehall and the Colonial Office, and managed to wangle a Constitutional Conference in 1964 attended by all active political parties and civil society where a date for Gambian independence was negotiated, signed and sealed for 18 February 1965.

Historians are quite unanimous in agreement with Jawara's pragmatic approach to independence. He knew the country was so ill-prepared for independence that it needed the goodwill and support of the British for a while even after independence. For example, literacy rate even in Bathurst was about 10 per cent at independence; the country's sole foreign exchange earner was groundnuts; there were less than five practicing doctors for the 300,000 Gambians and two high schools to prepare Gambians for university education abroad. Thus Berkeley Rice, the observant American reporter, coined the now infamous term 'improbable nation' to describe the newly independent nation.[124]

Indeed, at the very start of nationhood, the eyes of the world were on The Gambia, and no one seemed to have faith in the country's future survival as an independent state. Besides, maintaining close ties

---

[124] Rice, B. *Enter The Gambia: birth of an improbable nation*, Houdder and Stoughton, 1967.

with Britain, Jawara also developed a unique model of 'friendship with the world' where he shunned both the Communist and Capitalist appellations and adopted a non-aligned foreign policy, which is why he got assistance from the USSR, North Korea, Communist China bloc and the USA, UK, France bloc. In between, he wooed successfully the Arab world, including Gadaffi's Libya, which for example, established the first national bus service in 1976. Astute foreign policy became a tool for political survival under Jawara's 32 years in power.

Another tool for national development under Jawara's rule was his 'tesito' (self-help) philosophy. As early as the late 1960s, he and his Ministers were convinced of popular community participation in developing local infrastructure like classroom blocks, causeways, seed stores and similar rural infrastructures. By the mid-1970s, 'tesito' projects were animating the rural areas and there was a mass mobilisation of community talent and effort to build local infrastructure. Sadly, the good philosophy soon became politicised such that what was initially meant to mobilise national effort for nation building, became so much associated with the ruling PPP that opponents of the party disassociated themselves from 'tesito'.

Jawara also used his strong adherence to multi-party democracy and the rule of law to win friends and projects for the country. From 1962 to 1994, Jawara stubbornly stuck to a regular calendar of multiparty elections: 1962, 1966, 1972, 1977, 1982, 1987 and 1992; in between he organised two referenda in 1965 when he lost his bid to turn the country into a Republic and in 1970 when the 'yes' for Republican status won the day. Indeed, by 1972, Gambia was the only country in West Africa to be still holding regular multi-party elections, had no political prisoners and had an independent press, including a private radio station! Naomi Chazan and Robert Mortimer have described Gambia under Jawara as a 'pluralist regime' guided 'by a mixture of bargaining, compromise and reciprocity' with a 'notion of the separation of powers, multi-party political institution and a fairly vibrant representative structures'.[125]

This beautiful reputation earned us donors' money for national development projects in agriculture, roads and educational institutions such as Gambia College which opened in 1982, and the National Museum which opened in 1985 under the guidance of the leading historian Bakari Sidibe. Sadly, as the donor money poured in and state parastatals such as the Gambia Commercial Bank got established, corruption began to rear its ugly head in our body politic. It was apparent that Gambians were seeing less tangible results from the many donor funded projects strewn around the country. By the late 1970s, the Banjul courts were inundated with cases of alleged embezzlement by public servants, which tireless journalists like Pierre Sock, who wrote for the *Gambia Onward* newspaper, Baboucarr Gaye, stringer for the BBC, and Dixon Colley of the *Nation* newspaper reported on faithfully. At least

[125] See Chazan, N. &Robert Mortimer. *Politics and Society in Contemporary Africa*, Lynne Reiner Publishers, 1992, p.140-141.

action, however timid, was being taken and the public was being informed. Indeed, the only good news on the economic front at this time was the boom in tourists' arrivals and the completion of new hotels.

Even regrettable as it is, the 1981 coup attempt led by Kukoi Samba Sanyang (1953-2013)against Jawara's government in which a thousand Gambians died, property worth millions of dollars looted or destroyed and women raped, elicited a worldwide response of solidarity with Saudi Arabia alone donating US10 million towards the post-coup reconstruction effort; Gambians also contributed the equivalent of D30 million in cash and kind towards returning the country to normalcy.[126] Another result of the 1981 putsch was that it helped to seal the long awaited Senegambia Confederation which brought Senegal and Gambia together in a loose union which lasted from 1982-1989.

---

[126] See *Kairaba*, p.322

By the mid-1980s, the economy was atrophying due to internal issues of corruption, drought and also the world oil price hikes such that the country had to start a bitter Economic Recovery Programme. Although, it was touted as a success, its trail of massive sackings of public servants left a bitter taste in the mouths of many Gambians. This economic bitter pill and the apparent reluctance of Jawara to step aside for a younger cadre of leaders helped to clear the road for the July 22 1994 army coup which ousted him from power.

Jawara lives a quiet life in retirement outside Banjul.

Yahya A.J.J Jammeh (1965-)
President of The Gambia

President Jammeh has led The Gambia since 1994, following the military coup he led against the PPP regime of Sir Dawda Kairaba Jawara.

Immediately after he came to power as Chairman of the Armed Forces Provisional Ruling Council (AFPRC) on July 22 1994, he launched a programme of Rectification and Development which saw the establishment of numerous commissions to probe illicit earnings by members of the PPP regime. Running parallel to this programme of rectification was a massive infrastructure development project which occasioned the building of many schools, hospitals, roads and bridges in all parts of the country.

Aside from the numerous High Schools built, the AFPRC and its civilian corollary, the APRC, also established hospitals at Farafenni, Bwiam and

Serekunda. In 1997, a new Airport terminal was erected at Yundum, which has a capacity to handle a million passengers per year.

In 1995, University education was introduced into The Gambia with the establishment of the University Extension Programme run by St Mary's University in Canada. The first batch of Gambian local graduates passed out in a historic convocation held in February 1999, during which ceremony, Jammeh was given a Honorary Doctorate Degree from St Mary's University, one of many such awards he has garnered in recent years. A year later, The University of The Gambia was established which today has churned up hundreds of Gambian professionals including doctors, lawyers and teachers.

In 1996, Jammeh's government introduced a national TV Service which has since 2009 started broadcasting on satellite for worldwide audiences. The private media too has witnessed growth with over a dozen private FM radio stations and numerous private newspapers in circulation in spite of concerns expressed in some quarters about press freedom in the country. The introduction of GSM mobile services in 2001 has been so successful that over ninety per cent of Gambian adults have access to mobile phones.

In order to open up the Southern littoral to the rest of the country and to better tap its tourism potentials, the Kombo Coastal road was built in 2000, linking Southern Gambia to the Greater Banjul Area; in 2004, the North Bank road linking Barra and Jajanbureh was completed, fully macadamized. Bridges have been built across the Bao Bolong in the North Bank and at Jajanbureh linking the Island community to the South Bank.

In the political sphere, following the end of the two year transition from military rule in 1996, an Independent Electoral Commission was formed to oversee elections, which was quite a novel development as hitherto elections were organised and conducted by civil servants at the Electoral

Office of the Ministry of Local Government. Opposition parties in the first Republic criticised this arrangement as it did not lend weight to the credibility of elections. Other institutions created to contribute to participatory politics included the National Civic Education Commission and the Ombudsman. Gender and women's issues have received much attention also. Women have been represented in cabinet in multiple numbers since 1994, and there is a woman vice president in power since 1997. The Women's Act has been promulgated to further advance the lot of Gambian women in all spheres of life. Girls' enrolment in schools has increased dramatically in the past decade, so has their retention in school also improved thanks to the efforts of numerous stakeholders including the President's Girls Scholarships Scheme (PEGEP) which sponsors girls in school.

Another important development under his regime is the fact that Gambia has managed to diversify its foreign friends in the process winning economic and technical assistance from countries like Cuba, Venezuela, Iran and Taiwan. In the early 2000s, Gambia played a key role in brokering peace in Guinea Bissau and hosted many peace conferences dedicated to solving the insurgency in Casamance. To crown Gambia's foreign policy strides, the country hosted a successful African Union (AU) summit in 2006.

President Yahya Jammeh was born in Kanilai on 15 May 1965, and attended Gambia High School from 1978 to 1983. He enlisted into The Gambia National Gendamerie in 1984, and was commissioned in 1989. He joined the Gambia National Army and rose through the ranks, occupying positions such as security officer during the historic Pope John Paul visit to Banjul in 1992. Jammeh retired from the army as Colonel in 1996, to contest the elections as a civilian under the banner of the Alliance for Patriotic Re-orientation and Construction (APRC). He was re-elected as President in 2001, 2006, 2011 amidst stiff contest mounted by opposition leaders like Ousainou Darboe of the United Democratic

Party, Halifa Sallah of the Peoples' Democratic Organisation for Independence and Hamat Bah of the National Reconciliation Party. [127]

[127] In 2011 for example, Jammeh won over 72 percent of the votes cast.

Conclusion

The parade of eminent Gambians of the past two hundred years is completed, but not exhausted. I have in the foregoing, tried to confirm my premise that personalities indeed matter in the annals of a nation's history. In the life stories of the 40 or so Gambians profiled here, we can see also the outline of the historical evolution of the country over the past two centuries. From the text above, it is clear that Gambians have always had the courage to take the bull by the horn in defence of the interest of their country and people at the right and opportune time. Like true patriots, there have been men and women who braved the adversities imposed by man or nature to give their best for the country.

This is a moral lesson of history which readers and even non-readers of this book must bear in mind. Country must come first and last because it is all what we have as our own.

Historians should endeavour to hail the true and great achievements of Gambians so that our children will not be lost; groping for role models in foreign climes. Our country has produced and will surely continue to produce great men and women. The personal histories outlined above show that no effort towards nation building is small or insignificant. This is one powerful lesson of history as a discipline.

Finally, history is also a developmental and utilitarian discipline. It has a critical role to play in nation building. If properly studied, history could help us fight diseases such as malaria, AIDS; boost tourism; and empower the weak and marginalised.

History is above all a tool to help us recover our stolen past, identity and pride.

References

Archival Sources (files)

The Gambia National Archives, Banjul

CSO 2/978 'Domestic Science Scholarship for Miss Richards and Miss Fowlis'

CSO 2/2466 'The Women War Workers and Busy Bees'

CSO 2.814 Maternity and Child Welfare Committee'

CSO 2/1479 'Women Convicted of Capital Offences;

CSO 10/221 Widows and Orphans (Amendment)

CSO 2/2042 Overcrowding in Bathurst 1943'

CSO 2/1395 Age Limit for Marriage'

CSO 2/1652 Civil and Christian Marriages'

CSO 2/1695 Report on Methodist Girls High School'

CSO 2/1828 Registration of Mohammedans Marriages'

CSO 210/87 Venereal Diseases in Bathurst.

CSO 2/1798 'Ada Beigh'

CSO 2/2402 'Lady Education officer'

CSO 2/1395 'A minimum age for marriage'

LGO 1/24 'Women's Education'

Published Sources

Newspapers and Magazines

1. *The Gambia Echo*, Bathurst, 1930-1965
2. *The Gambia News Bulletin*, Bathurst, 1944-1965
3. *The Gambia Outlook*, Bathurst 1930-1946
4. *The Vanguard*, Bathurst, 1958-1959
5. *West Africa magazine*, London, 1917-2006
6. *Women Today*, London, 1960
7. *Africa Women*, London, 1960
8. *The Crown Colonist*, London, 1944
9. *New Commonwealth*, London, 1966
10. *The Gambia Daily Observer*, 1992- to date
11. *Topic Magazine, Gambia, 1989-1991*

Books and Articles

Amadiume, Ifi. (1987), *Male Daughters, Female Husbands*, London: Zed books.

Awe, Bolanle. (1977), 'The Iyolade in the traditional Yoruba System; in A. Schogel (ed) *Sexual Stratification: a cross cultural view*, Columbus: Columbia University Press.

Carney, Judith. (2001), *Black Rice,*Harvard: Harvard University Press.

Cocquery-Vidrovitch. (1997), *African Women: a modern History*, New york: Westview Press.

Ceesay, Hassoum. (2007). *Gambian Women: And Introductory History*, Kanifing: Fulladu Publishers.

Ceesay, Hassoum. (2012). *Gambian Women: Profiles and Historical Notes, Kanifing: Fulladu Publishers.*

Ceesay, Hassoum. 'Chiefs and Protectorate Administration in Colonial Gambia (1894-1965) in *Leadership In Colonial Africa*, Baba G Jallow (ed), Macmillan Palgrave, 2014.

Chazan, N. And Robert Mortimer. *Politics and Society in Contemporary Africa,* Lynne Reiner Publishers, 1992.

(Ed), (20014), London: Macmillan Palgrave.

Diop, Cheikh Anta. (1989), *The Cultural Unity of Black Africa*, London,: Karnak Press.

Dogbe, E. (2002), 'Visibility, Eloquence and Silence: Women and theatre for Development in Ghana', in Martin Barnham (ed) *African theatre: Women,* James Currey, London.

Frederiks, Martha. (2004), *We have toiled all night: a history of Christianity in The Gambia 1456-2004,* Leiden: Boekcentrum.

Gamble, David P. (2007), *A Review of Development Schemes in The Gambia,* the author, Brisbane, CA. (2007), *Review of Development Projects in the Gambia in the colonial period,* Brisbane, CA. (1985), *The Peoples of The Gambia: Wollof,* the author, Brisbane: CA.

Gamble, David P. and P E H Hair (eds). *(2001), The Discovery of the River Gambia by Richard Jobson (1623),* The Haklyut Society.

Gardiner, Juliet (ed). (1988), *What is History,* London: Macmillan.

Geiger, S. 1986, 'Tanganyikan Nationalism as Women's Work', *Journal of African History.*

Gray, John M. (1940), *A History of The Gambia,* London: Frank Cass.

Gray, William. (1825), *Travels in Africa,* London

Grey-Johnson, Nana. (2002), *EF Small: the Watchdog of Society,* Banjul: BPMRU.

Grey-Johnson, Nana. (2002), *EF Small, The Watchdog of Society,* Banjul: BPMRU.

Hughes, Arnold & David Perfect. (2006), *A Political History of The Gambia,* Rochester: Rochester University Press.

Hughes, Arnold and David Perfect, (2008), *Historical Dictionary of The Gambia,* Scarecrow Press.

Hodgson, Dorothy L. (2001), *'Wicked' Women and the Reconfiguration of gender in Africa,* Heinemann, London.

Jawara, Augusta. (1965), 'Gambia Women's Federation' in *Africa Woman Today.*

Jawara, Alhaji Sir Dawda (2010), *Kairaba: autobiography,* Domtom Publishers, London.

Little , Kenneth. (1973), *African women in towns,* London: Cambridge University Press.

Mark., Peter. *(2002), 'Portuguese style' and Luso-African Identity: Pre-colonial Senegambia,* Indiana: Indiana University Press.

Oliver, Caroline. (1982), *Western Women in Colonial Africa,* London: Greenwood Press.

Mahoney, Florence. (1974), *Stories of Senegambia,* Bathurst: Government Printer.

PPP Secretariat, (1992), *The Story of the PPP,* Banjul: Baroueli.

Harris, J. (1916), 'War Contributions from Africa', *Journal of the Royal African Society*

Illife, John. (2000), *Africans: a history of a continent,* Cambridge: University Press.

Roberts, J.M. (1982), *Europe 1880-1945,* London: Longman.

Akyeampong, Emmanuel and Henry Louis Gates Jr. (eds). *Dictionary of African Biography,* Oxford: Oxford University Press, 2012.

Oxford University Press. *African American Studies Center,* edited by Ed. . *Oxford African*

American Studies Center, 'http://www.oxfordaasc.com/article/opr/t356/e0049 (accessed Fri Feb 14 14:24:32 EST 2014).

Rodney, Walter. (1982), *How Europe Underdeveloped Africa,* Washington D.C.: Harvard University Press.

Senghor, Jeggan. (2014), *The Reverend J C Faye: His Life and Times, London: AuthorHouse.*

Sonko Godwin, Patience. (1987), *Ethnic Groups of the Senegambia*, Banjul: BPMRU.

Swindell, Ken. (1977), 'Migrant farmers in The Gambia' *Journal of African History.*

Tripp, Aili Mari. (2005), 'Women in Movement', in *Readings in Gender in Africa,* Andrea Cornwall (ed) London: James Currey.

Other books by Global Hands Publishing

Gendered Voices From The Gambia (2015)
Pierre Gomez and Isatou Ndow

This book contributes and builds on the growing academic literature on gender. It draws on a number of Gambian works to analyse gender in contemporary Gambian fiction.

It focuses on challenging the social construction of gender norms, inequality and abuse whilst analysing how gender norms and stereotypes are represented, reinforced and challenged in significant facets of Gambian literature.

A great insightful and thought provoking read for students, scholars and lay persons interested in African literature, gender studies and Gambian studies.

Harrow: London Poems of Convalescence (2014)

Tijan M. Sallah

Harrow: London Poems of Convalescence is a unique collection of poems. Rhyming, simple and reflective, they depart from the poet's usual free verse. The poems deal with the near-death experience of a pedestrian hit by a car in London, the agony of pain in recovery and finally, the magic of healing.

It is poetry geared towards a private function, quite unlike his other poems, which extol either Gambian Wolof values or criticize American racism and materialism.

Harvest of Gambian Lines: An Anthology of Poems (2014)
Edited by Abdoulie Jatta and Musa Jallow

An anthology of poems that envision multiplications of until it dispels grief and returns the lost exuberant pride. These poems offer a vision of the world beyond the physical sense, where the seed of peace germinates and breaks into leaf to line the walls of faith and selfhood. This is an anthology that demonstrates what happens when writing is dedicated to socio-political and economical changes; particularly concerning the issues that many Africans face: debt; religiosity; poverty; venality of rulers and the betrayal and threat to innocence.

These poets bear witness to the interior landscape of the cellular workshop of their very beings.

The Graveyard Cannot Pray (2013)

Baba Galleh Jallow

This book is an autobiographical account of one man's battle to save his daughter from female circumcision. A struggle that is defiant of a harmful traditional practice and defective constructions of normality. This is perhaps the first autobiographical account of a male perspective articulating to battle against Female Genital Mutilation. The Graveyard Cannot Pray throws into sharp relief four interconnected phenomena: the conflict between an older and younger generation; the communal nature of conflict and resolution among the Futa Fulani; the Fulani notion of son-hood, and the potential complications that arise when the sanctity of tradition is stood in opposition against the sanctity of faith.

Innocent Questions (2012)

Momodou Sallah

This collection of poems harnesses the theme of struggle in a way very few writers have been able to. The author combines his background of growing up in The Gambia and an adult life residing in the UK to great effect: a fusion of writing styles and constructed realities.

The poems in this collection jump from the pages and evoke palpable emotions. This collection of thirty two poems explores a range of pertinent issues with a complex simplicity that is dramatic and mesmerising; from the dreams of an African schoolboy to the frustrations of a consummate professional in Babylon.

Lightning Source UK Ltd.
Milton Keynes UK
UKOW04f0052231215
265231UK00001B/16/P

www.ingramcontent.com/pod-product-compliance
Ingram Content Group UK Ltd.
Pitfield, Milton Keynes, MK11 3LW, UK
UKHW040023200726
13854UKWH00001B/321